MY ADDICT YOUR ADDICT

Testimonials:

From Addicts:

"Jack saved my life."

"He explained it to me like nobody ever has."

"He was the first person in my life to ask me if I wanted help."

"He had faith in me even when I didn't have faith in myself."

"It was as if he could see inside my soul."

"Jack is real... he's been there... he's done it. He knows what it takes."

"I met Jack in 1999. He taught me a lot and helped me and my family a great deal."

"I feel like I have purpose in my life today and I owe it all to Jack."

"Jack Levine really cares about people."

"As a recovering addict himself, he can reach people who are otherwise unreachable."

"Jack was able to cut through the denial of addiction."

From Parents:

"You taught me how to live again."

"You took my guilt away."

"As a parent he could relate first hand to my pain and desperation."

From Professionals:

"Jack knows from his own experience the pain and misery that addiction creates in both the addict and the entire family unit. His new program is a great resource in helping people to overcome their addiction."

— Rehab Center executive

"Jack's impact on our team was significant and immediate. The passion he brings persuades people to react and change immediately. Great results!"

— Willie Romeo, Former Burger King Marketing Director

Overcome Any Addiction Now

MY ADDICT YOUR ADDICT

Jack Alan Levine

My Addict, Your Addict
By Jack Alan Levine

Published by Great Hope Publishing, Coconut Creek, Fl

www.LifeSolutionSeminars.com
www.GreatHopePublishing.com
www.JackAlanLevine.com

Email us at: connect@LifeSolutionSeminars.com

ISBN 978-0-9825526-5-0
Library of Congress Control Number: 2014933078

Dedication

I want to dedicate this book to everyone who has encouraged me and inspired me to make sure this book would get written, and that my *Free For Life at Last: Overcoming Addiction* online video program would get produced. It is my hope and the deep prayer of my heart and so many others I know, that we can continue to reach out and help those who are suffering from addiction, to help them break free and to live the life that God intended them to live... a life full of hope, joy and peace... a life full of excitement, adventure, purpose, knowledge, wisdom and happiness. I know of no better things for anyone and, Lord knows, I've tried everything else!

Disclaimers

LIFE SOLUTION SEMINARS LLC and Jack Alan Levine, together with their contractors, employees, agents, representatives and heirs, (hereinafter LIFE SOLUTIONS and/or Jack Alan Levine and/or Free For life At Last Overcoming Addiction Program and/or Website and/or LifeSolutionSeminars.com) is an informational book. The resources made available by LIFE SOLUTIONS in this Book are provided for informational purposes only, and should not be used to replace the specialized training and professional judgment of a health care or mental health care professional. In addition, LIFE SOLUTIONS makes no representations or warranties and expressly disclaims any and all liability concerning any treatment or action by any person following the information offered or provided within or through the book. Nothing you see or read anywhere in this book is meant to diagnose, substitute for, or otherwise replace actual face-to-face professional counseling. Neither LIFE SOLUTIONS nor any of their employees, agents, representatives or assigns is responsible for any action taken by any person as a result of reading or otherwise obtaining information from this book. LIFE SOLUTIONS cannot be held responsible for the use of the information provided. Please always consult a physician or a trained mental health professional before making any decision regarding treatment of yourself or others and BEFORE using this book. The primary goal for establishing this book is to educate and compassionately support its reader. This book does not provide the information on these pages to substitute for individualized therapies. No claim to cure, treat, diagnose or otherwise provide mental or behavioral healthcare is guaranteed promised or implied by this book. No legal or other professional services are being rendered and nothing is intended to provide such services or advice of any kind. LIFE SOLUTIONS cannot and will not provide treatment through this book or over the Internet and LIFE SOLUTIONS does not have an ongoing private therapeutic practice. All rights reserved.

For any additional information, please contact:
LIFE SOLUTION SEMINARS LLC
6574 North State Road 7, #277
Coconut Creek, FL 33073

Table of Contents

Acknowledgments
Preface

Part I: MY STORY

Part II: RICKY'S STORY

Part III: THE WAY OUT

Part IV: FREE FOR LIFE-OVERCOMING ADDICTION

ACKNOWLEDGMENTS

I want to thank my wife, Beth, who has always stood beside me in our 13 years of marriage, and supported me and encouraged me on every single project I've done. But none is more important to her heart than this project, as she too is a recovering addict, now sober for over 30 years. Thank you, honey, for your time and effort in proofreading this book and your comments and suggestions, which were extremely helpful. But most importantly thank you always for believing in me, and God's purpose for my life, and sacrificing to make that a reality. You are awesome and I love you.

A special, heartfelt thanks to my editor, John Rabe, who worked tirelessly on this project, as he has on many of my books, always diving in headfirst with excitement and enthusiasm, and giving his all to ensure that the product you read is the best it possibly can be. I'm grateful to John, and to his family, for allowing him to take time away from them in order to accomplish this mission. We both believe it will be a great blessing to others. Not only is John a trusted friend and an amazing editor, but he is also a Springsteen fan, which pretty much makes him the perfect person. (Smile!)

I want to thank Shaun Smith, whose desire to see people live a better quality life was the inspiration for our mission statement which is simply "to help people live better personal and professional lives through online video programs and live seminars." Shaun's devotion to our mission is inspiring to me. I know the greatest joy he gets is seeing that we impacted someone's life in a positive way and helped them live a better life. That's just one of the many reasons he's such a blessing to me.

This book is written for every person who's ever suffered from any addiction. If you are still suffering from any addiction, the purpose of the book is to let you know there is hope, there is an answer, and there is a way out! Just as importantly, this book is for every family member or friend who has a loved who is struggling with addiction. We need to make sure you don't let your loved ones addiction ruin your life. Finally, if you are like me and my wife, and you have victory over your addiction, then you know as well as I do how critical it is that we keep on helping those in need. We must remember by giving it away we get to keep it. We must take to heart our mission, which is helping other people who are suffering and in need with the strength, experience and hope that we ourselves have experienced from God. On that note, it is my pleasure and joy to give you this book.

Preface

My name is Jack Alan Levine. I am an author, businessman and speaker, but this book is not about my professional life, it is about addiction. I'm here more to tell you about my personal life. My hope is to share my personal experiences in ways that will bless you, help you and change your life forever.

I've gone through drug addiction and I've gone through gambling addiction. I've counseled thousands of people over the years who have gone through the same, and I know what a torturous life it can be to be caught up in that kind of addiction. It's an awful thing. I've experienced it in my own life and I've experienced it as a parent, as I watched my son struggle with addiction for years (it started when he was 18).

Whether you are in the throes of addiction yourself or seeing a loved one suffer through it, I can help you. I have results and solutions for real-life situations that can crystallize this for you. Each person's situation is different, but the root is the same for everybody. Through my own story, I can tell you what the choices are, the impacts of those choices, the results of those choices, and what sacrifices you'll have to make to get where you want to be.

If you're like me, you know you need to be free for life, forever, done with addiction, and not having it ruin your life, not having it control your life. I know what it's like to be controlled by addiction. I know what it's like to feel I'm in the pit of Hell, to feel that Satan's got me and he won't let go. It's a horrible feeling. When you are in the grip of an addiction, it affects everybody and everything around you. It affected me, it affected my family, my friends, my work, my health, my finances, and my marriage... every single part of my life.

What I want to do is tell you my story and the stories of some of the people I love, to show you there is hope. There is a way out. My story is not always pretty. Sometimes it's funny. Sometimes it's horrifying. But it's always real and I'm a testimony to the reality that addiction *can* be defeated.

I can share with you some basic things I've learned about the mechanics of addiction along the way, but this book is only a small starting point. I believe when you are done reading and we've spent our time together, you will be pointed in the direction of some possible solutions. Beyond this book, I have more material that can help you step-by-step, including my in-depth *Free For Life at Last: Overcoming Addiction* online video program, and my *Life Solution* Seminars.

I designed this book to be read quickly. I don't want you to get bogged down in a long, drawn out read. You'll see what an addict looks like, discover how they think, and get some basic insights on how it can be overcome. My purpose here is to give you a bird's-eye view, no matter in which part of the addiction spiral you've found yourself in, to help you see, through my story, my son's story, and the things I've learned along the way, there is a way out of addiction.

I want to hear from you. Write to me. E-mail me. I want to hear your stories because I'm always looking to grow and to find more ways to help people.

Jack Alan Levine

PART I
MY STORY

1
BEGINNINGS

I was brought up in a middle class family in Yonkers, New York. I had very loving parents, which may not always be the case with addicts. But I'm proof that addiction can cut through every demographic, geographic, or psychographic profile you can possibly imagine. Addicts can be businessmen, bums, teachers, housewives, students. *All* types of people suffer from addiction. Addiction is not about the type of person you are, or about your station in life; it's about what happens to you.

In a way, addiction is like a hurricane. Think how silly it would be to say, "Well, there's a hurricane coming, but it's only going to hit the white people who are 40 years old." No! It's going to hit everybody in its way. That's what addiction is. It simply cuts across America leaving wreckage in its path.

So, there I was in this middle class, wonderful family, with loving parents who spoiled my brother and me rotten. We lived a great life! We went to Yankee games and had birthday bowling parties. I did well in school and everything was good. At about 16 years old, I really, really started to desire to live a different kind of life. What I mean is, I'd always been a good kid, but I started to see that the bad kids were getting away with a lot of stuff that seemed pretty cool to me.

I was in ninth grade and thought, "I need to see what the other side is like." So I made a conscious effort to join these other kids, and most of them didn't have the upbringing I had. I had a strong family system and parental love, but they had something... something *else* I wanted. They had *freedom* – or so I thought.

So I started hanging out with a different crowd. As you can probably guess, one thing led to another, and I tried marijuana for the first time.

[This would be a good time to tell you, by the way, that while addiction itself is not funny at all, many of my experiences along the way have been quite comical, as you'll see.]

The first time I tried marijuana, I didn't feel any effects at all. The second time I tried it, I didn't feel any effects. The third, fourth and fifth times, still nothing! I'll never forget my friends taking me out into the woods day after day for a *week*, continuing to ply me with marijuana. Finally, about the seventh or eighth day, I felt it. The problem on all those other days was I didn't know what effect I was looking for. I didn't recognize it. Eventually, after doing it and doing it, and having my friends explain what it was supposed to feel like, I felt the effect. And let me tell you, I would have been much better off had I not come back for days two, three, four, five, six, seven and eight, for the marijuana. I've heard many people scoff at the notion that marijuana is a "gateway drug," a drug that opens the door for addiction to harder drugs. Well, for me, it absolutely was. Little did I know that those daily tokes out in the woods were the beginning of a path to self-destruction.

Once I started to really feel the effects of the pot, it was great. *I loved it.* I smoked pot for years after that. I can remember literally smoking pot every morning on our way to high school. And we'd have so much fun. We thought we knew everything.

Now, it's important to understand something as an addict, or as a parent of an addict, or as a spouse or loved one of an addict: in the beginning, drugs are often unbelievably fun and awesome. It's not like they're terrible in the beginning, but they suck you in over time. The way they suck you in is a *tragedy*. Think of a stranger offering you candy to come and get in the car with him so he can kidnap you to do who knows what to you. That's what the drugs are. They look great from the outside. Then you get them. You put the candy in your mouth. You go, "Wow! This candy is delicious. I should hang out with this guy a little more!" Then he has his hooks in you. Drugs are the *stranger* in the car dangling candy in front of you, it's not a good path to go down.

But down the path I went.

2
COLLEGE

I partied through the rest of high school then, when I went off to college, I got *really* serious about partying. I partied my brains out. I began pursuing a "higher" education, if you will. I graduated from marijuana to Quaaludes and other barbiturates, which I loved.

Now, everybody's metabolism is different. I never liked "speedy" drugs, for the most part (except for cocaine, which we'll get to shortly). I usually liked drugs that slowed me down and made me feel the best – Percocet, Quaaludes, barbiturates, pain killers of all kinds.

My friends and I went through college smoking pot all the time, taking Quaaludes all the time, and you know what? We made the serious mistake of often mixing alcohol with some of those, as well. By the way, just so we're clear, there is no difference between alcohol, cocaine, marijuana, Quaaludes, Percocet, Halcion, Xanax, Crystal Meth, Ecstacy, speed, or LSD. You can get addicted to any of them very easily.

Xanax wasn't around back in that day, but Valium was all over the place. I remember once driving from New York to Florida taking Valium the whole way down. I was taking five milligram Valiums every hour. You say, how can that be? How could you not crash? Well, you build up a tolerance. You build up a resistance. As I tell you stories that might shock you, (though an addict won't be shocked – they understand exactly how this works) it's important for me to tell you that it's not the *quantity* of drugs that make you an addict. It's *never* about the *quantity*.

Later when I was in recovery at a Narcotics Anonymous meeting, I met this big motorcycle guy, with the bushy beard, the headscarf, the leather vest and chains. He asked me what my "drug of choice" was, which is an addict's phrase. Mine was Percocet at the time (along with a little cocaine), which I told him.

"How many do you take?" he asked me.

"Well, I used to take three a day, one every three or four hours. Then it got so bad, I got up to six a day."

He looked at me and he laughed. "Oh yeah?" he said. "Well I took 40 a day!" He told me he'd gotten so messed up from Percocet (a prescription painkiller) that he cut his finger off, which he then showed me.

The point is, his addiction and tolerance had built him up to the level that he could do 40 Percocet a day. If you're not an addict, you'd probably be wiped out by two. But he could do 40 a day because he had built up a tolerance.

A few years ago, the conservative talk radio host Rush Limbaugh came out as an Oxycodone addict. He was eventually charged, after an investigation, with "doctor shopping" where he got a bunch of doctors to write him overlapping prescriptions for painkillers – at one point, according to news reports, about 2000 pills in a six-month period. It was said he sometimes took dozens of pills a day. People were amazed when they heard the reports of how much he'd taken. If you were to start from zero and take, say, a dozen painkillers, you would likely be dead in a day. Yet during Limbaugh's addiction, he continued hosting a daily radio program with 20 million listeners across the nation! You build up a tolerance where you need more and more just to keep the effect going. As an addict, I understood that.

3
ENTREPRENEUR

S o, I was taking drugs left and right in college, at Syracuse University. Then I took another big step I'm not
very proud of. I'm in my 50's now, but I was 18 and
foolish then, and I saw an opportunity to make big money. I
started to *sell* drugs, first pot and later cocaine. There were
other kids on the campus who were selling drugs, and one
day I met one of the bigger dealers on campus. This guy and
I became friends one night. We were at a party doing cocaine
together, and I said, "Let me ask you a question. How much
money are you making?"

I wanted to compare how he was doing with how I was
doing. The money had started pouring in – there was no lack
of people looking for drugs on the campus of a major university in the late 1970's. At one point I had $28,000 stashed away
in a safe deposit box. I knew he had to be raking in money
too; the only question was how much. I was curious to see if
he was making more than I was. After all, money was the only
reason to do this. Buying and using was one thing, but why
would you sell them and take the risk of doing jail time unless
you were going to make serious money?

He looked at me and he said, "Oh, I don't make money.
I just do it for the stash; to have my own drugs." I thought,
man, you're like the stupidest man in the world. That incident
inflated my sense of pride. I thought, "Oh, Jack, what a great
businessman you are!" Yeah, and my industry was drugs.

I was making tremendous money for a college kid selling
pot. But there was more to be had.

One day, I was playing softball at the college. This one guy
was hanging around watching, so I asked him if he wanted

to play and he said, yeah. After the game, we chatted, and it turned out his brother was from the Bronx and had this amazing cocaine connection. Amazing how quickly we got to that subject. So, with a connection in place, I started selling – and doing – cocaine.

4
COCAINE

Let me tell you something about cocaine. During the first three to six months I used cocaine, there was absolutely no doubt in my mind whatsoever that if everyone in the world, and all the world leaders, sat down and did lines of cocaine, there would be world peace. I was 100 percent convinced of that. I believed there would never be a problem in the world again. War? Solved. World hunger? A thing of the past. Why? Because when I did the cocaine, everything seemed so crystal clear to me. I had (or thought I had) vision, clarity, an intense insight into life and its intricacies I'd never had before. It was amazing – for a very short period of time. For six months, maybe eight months, maybe even a year.

Then, the tide turned.

You know how momentum shifts in a sporting event? Being from New York, I grew up a Yankees fan. For decades, the Yankees won championship after championship, while their archrivals, the Boston Red Sox, hadn't won a World Series in 86 years. In 2004 they were playing each other in the League Championship Series for the right to go to the World Series. The Yankees led the series 3-1, and only needed one more win to put the Sox away yet again.

But baseball fans remember what happened. Game Four went into the bottom of the 9th inning with the Yankees leading 4-3, and their Hall of Fame-caliber closer, Mariano Rivera, came in to close out the game – and the series – for the Yanks. Game over, right? But Mariano uncharacteristically walked the leadoff guy, and little-known speedster named Dave Roberts was brought in to pinch-runner him at first base. Everyone in the park *knew* Roberts was going to try to steal second. Mariano Rivera knew it. The Yankees catcher knew it. The hot dog vendors knew it.

Rivera threw over to first several times to keep Roberts close. On the first pitch to the batter, Roberts took off and stole second. You could just *feel* everything suddenly shift. The Yankees were three outs away from winning the series, but the whole feeling just went *whoosh*. The game and its momentum had changed in an instant.

The Red Sox won that night – and then won the next three straight to eliminate the Yankees on the way to winning their first World Series since 1918.

The momentum shift was just like that for me with cocaine, quick and disastrous. In the blink of an eye it transformed from being this amazing drug, able to give me enlightenment and insight, into a terrifying, life-sucking tragedy of a drug that now owned and controlled me. It no longer made me outgoing and insightful. It made me paranoid and crazy. Let me tell you something, there is no worse feeling I know than coming down from a cocaine high. Not a worse feeling in the entire world that I know – which is probably the reason that I don't do it today. I never want to experience that again as long as I live.

Don't get me wrong. I'm not sitting here telling you that I don't like the effects of drugs. I *do* like the good effects of drugs. What I am telling you is I hate is what happens *afterward*. The coming down... The depths of that pain and depression... The pure suffering... And it's not just physical withdrawal. There's an intense, indescribable emotional pain that comes with coming down. It was horrific.

So I can tell you that, like a lot of other addicts, I went on binges – three days, five days, at a time, staying up, doing cocaine. Then, the older I got, the longer it took me to recover. In college, we'd party all night. It'd take me a day to recover, maybe two. Then I got older, into my late 20's, and it would take me a week to recover from two nights of partying.

It took an amazing physical and mental toll. I went from an outgoing extrovert who wanted to talk to everybody and solve the world's problems, to a man literally hiding in the closets because I thought the cops were right outside my door. I was paranoid of every sound, every bird, every barking dog...

One story will give you a pretty good idea of what it looked like. We heard rumors that there were cops – or "narcs" as we called them – on campus. Not a good thing. I think we were sophomores at the time, and who wanted to get arrested? There was a security guard in our dorm who we were leery of because he always wanted to come up to our rooms and smoke pot with us. We never let him because we always suspected he might be a narc. There was a lot of that kind of thinking. "Who's the narc?" We could never be sure.

One night, I was calling out for a pizza. Then, my diet was a lot like a normal college kid. I called Domino's just about *every night* for pizza. So, one night I called and ordered pizza. I don't know what the guy on the other end of the phone said to me. It must've been something like, "We'll be there in 35 minutes." or "Can you repeat that order?" or something similarly mundane; but whatever he said triggered my paranoia. I was absolutely sure, at that very moment in time, I had figured it out: *The Domino's guys were the narcs!*

It made perfect sense. They were outside our dorm buildings in delivery trucks. They were regularly up in our dorm rooms. They could have been taping all our calls! They knew who we were! My paranoia was running crazy. I was like, "It's the Domino's guys! It's the Domino's guys!"

Terrified, I hung up the phone. I ran to tell my roommate.

"George! George! I figured it out! It's the Domino's guys! They're the narcs! They're coming! They're coming to arrest us! I'm sure of it! I'm sure of it! It's all over. It's the Domino's guys. We're dead."

George, who was this big, calm guy from Boston, looked at me.

"Jack, I'll tell you what," he said, "Why don't you go to Ian and Henry's room and wait there, and I'll wait for the Domino's guys." Ian and Henry were our friends who lived up on the third floor.

"That's an excellent idea, George!" I babbled. "You are a genius! That's exactly what I'm going to do. You stay here and get busted. I'm going upstairs to the third floor."

I ran upstairs, shaking like a leaf.

About 40 minutes later, there was a knock on Ian and Henry's door. Before I could even protest or dive into a hiding place, one of the guys opened the door. I was beside myself. "This is it. It's all over!" I thought.

There was my roommate George, standing in the doorway.

"Jack," he said, with more than a hint of a grin on his face, "Pizza's here."

If you're using cocaine, you have some stories of your own about being paranoid. You don't even have to tell them to me –

I *know* that's the case. I've been there, I get it, I understand it, both the fun and the misery.

It's mindboggling to me how stupid my friends and I could be with drugs. Many times, I would simply disappear. One time in college, I disappeared for two nights. My girlfriend thought I was dead. She called the police, and they were out looking for me. When I finally showed up, I told her, "Oh, I just spent the night at the park." She knew I was full of crap, but she didn't call me on it.

Another time in college, my mother was having an operation, so I went from Syracuse to Westchester (about a 4 ½ hour drive) to see her. My father was so happy I had shown up to encourage my mother.

And then I disappeared for three days on a cocaine binge.

Instead of doing something wonderful, instead of being there to support my mother, I had everyone panicked and worried about me, while my mother was lying there in the hospital for surgery. Nobody could find me.

At the end of the three days, when I showed my face again, my father just looked at me and shook his head. He wouldn't even say a word. I never felt lower. I never felt more worthless in my life.

I didn't want to hurt them, or worry them, or disappoint them. I would get lost in one of those binges. During it, you can't call someone and say, "Hey, I'm okay, don't worry about me." You can't even get the words out of your mouth. You can't even pick up the phone. You're in your own world and mind. Of course there were no cell phones then. If only there had been, I could have just texted I was OK. I would have saved everyone a lot of pain, worry and aggravation. But no such luck in the 70's.

The collegiate insanity didn't end there. I remember once taking pills that somebody gave me without even knowing what they were. I just popped them in my mouth and gulped them down. I mean, how stupid is that? I swallowed them, and then found myself driving to Vernon Downs, about 45 minutes from campus, where I used to regularly visit to feed *another* addiction – gambling. (More on that shortly.) Suddenly I started having really strange feelings from the pills, and it became a very, very bad situation. As I was driving, I saw the dreaded flashing lights in my rearview mirror. I pulled over and sat waiting in fear. The cop strolled up to my window and immediately figured out – which wasn't that tough to do – that something was seriously off.

My buddy George was with me in the car, and the cops pulled us out, cuffed us, and took us to the police station. Needless to say, I was terrified. I thought, "Oh my gosh, it's all over. They're going to call my parents. I'll get thrown out of school. This is horrible."

We sat there in this little police station in Vernon, New York and the cop was playing Tough Cop with me, rightfully so, and I was scared. I had not officially crapped in my pants yet, but I was close.

The cop sat across the desk, and he started hammering George and me about what we were doing. He was letting us *have it*. There was no way this situation was going to end well. My life was going to be ruined.

Out of nowhere, the phone rang, interrupting the cop in mid-tirade. He grudgingly stopped to answer it, and what do you know? It's a robbery call. Somebody else's terrible night just became the best news I could've gotten. The cop had to go out on a robbery call. In disgust, with no other available options, he looked at the other cop there and spit, with disgust, "Just write them a ticket and let them go."

I thought, "Man, how lucky are we? *How lucky are we*?" I might've done a celebration dance if I didn't think it would've gotten me locked up for life!

In reality, it was yet another warning sign that things in my life were bad and headed for worse.

Another time, I remember coming back on a bus ride from Boston with another buddy of mine. Through a roommate's friends back home, we'd met these guys who were big, big pot dealers. As a result, we were bringing *seven pounds* of pot back from Boston to Syracuse in our luggage. It was a big deal. This was dangerous stuff.

As we were riding back, my friend pulled out a joint and lit up right in the back of the bus. Now you might think that this is not the most intelligent behavior when you have seven pounds of pot in your luggage – and you would be exactly right. But we were young. We were stupid. We didn't care. So my friend fired up a joint and I said, "Um…that's probably not a good idea." He says, "No, no, no. No problem." Obviously he was no genius either.

The bus driver pulled over, stopped the bus, unbuckled himself, and stormed back to where we were sitting.

"If I smell any more marijuana, the state troopers will meet us at the next stop," he said, with no small amount of anger. I can only imagine what the other passengers on the bus thought. We brought the seven pounds back and we made a lot of money, which was part of the appeal of it all.

5
GAMBLING

I started gambling at 13. My buddies and I had this neighbor lady, Ellen, who would take us to the bingo halls with her on Thursday nights. There we'd be, this pack of young teenage boys in there with our cards and our ink stampers playing Bingo with the old ladies. It might not sound like much fun, but the thrill of winning, the excitement of the big score, needing just one more number for the big win, was intoxicating to me.

From bingo with the little old ladies, I advanced to horse racing. My father took me to Yonkers Raceway when I was 16 years old to see the first horse race of my life. I remember like it was yesterday. My dad let me buy a ticket, and not knowing a thing about racing, I put two bucks down on the number three horse, for the win.

At the sound of the bell, my horse charged out of the starting gate and I watched him pace around the track. My horse, the number three horse, was running neck-and-neck with the five horse. They were as close as they could be when they crossed the line in a photo finish. I couldn't believe it! I was dying with anticipation as the results were checked. Then it was announced: the five horse beat my three horse by a nose.

It didn't bother me that I lost. I remember saying to my father, "Let me get this right. If I had had the five horse, I would've just won $14?" He said, "Yeah, that's right." I was hooked *instantly*. It was like mainlining heroin into my arm. From the very first race, I was hooked on gambling. I absolutely loved it. In short time, I graduated from horse racing to betting on sports to betting in casinos.

For those of you who haven't experienced it in the same way, I want you to understand what it means to be obsessed and compulsive about something. I remember going to Yonkers Raceway one night with $300 in my pocket – which, by the way, was a lot of money for a 17 year old to have at that time. I had $600 or $700 saved up at home in my closet, and I drove the 15 minutes from my house to Yonkers Raceway that night with $300 of it, and lost it. Did I stop there? That's not how it works with addiction. Instead, positive that I had a sure thing in the ninth race, I zoomed back home, took another $300 out of my closet, and drove back to the track to put it on that race. Needless to say, I lost that too.

I can remember sitting in my bed many, many nights listening to the crackling AM radio, waiting for the West Coast scores to come in on basketball or baseball, with all my happiness and joy being totally dependent on whether I won or lost those games.

I remember one summer when I was a senior in high school, I was down almost two thousand dollars to the bookie I bet with, and I didn't have the money. Anybody who's ever watched a movie knows what happens when you owe a bookie big money and you can't pay. That's not a good situation, financially or physically!

The realization came to me: I was going to have to tell my father, and ask him for the money. I was in real trouble. That was going to be a difficult conversation, but it was the sensible thing to do. But the thought was agonizing to me. I felt like my secret would be discovered. I felt like my world was going to come crashing down. My dad had specifically warned me about gambling. He told me about some issues with gambling he'd had in his own life, and about how he overcame it. He told me how used to shoot craps as a kid in the subway, but that he realized there was no future in it.

"Don't do it," he said. "Don't stick your hand in the fire, Jack. It's hot."

Like most arrogant kids, I thought I knew it all. "No, Dad. It's not hot. You must've been mistaken when you stuck your own hand in. Maybe you just didn't know how to do it right," I thought. Yeah, right.

So instead I rethought my plan, and did the only thing a good, addictive gambler would do – I went double or nothing on the Mets. I remember the Mets were playing the Pirates. It was a Sunday afternoon. It was the last day of the betting week, which goes from Monday to Sunday. Jon Matlack was pitching for the Mets, and I was sitting out by the pool listening to it. I died a thousand times that day. I remember thinking over and over, "This is the end of my life. This is the last three hours of freedom I'll ever have." I can't tell you the torture, pitch by pitch, out by out, I went through sitting by that pool.

Incredibly enough, the Mets (and I) won that game, taking my hide out of the fire for the time being. The relief was amazing; it was like I had been given a new lease on life. It was probably also the worst thing that could've ever happened to me, because it enabled me to continue gambling rather than admit my problem and get help.

The gambling continued, and I remember having multiple thousands dollar bets on basketball games, baseball games, football games – You name it, I bet it. At 21, 22 years old, remember, I was making money in college selling drugs. So, I had money to bet and gamble. My addictions were beginning to feed each other.

6
MADISON AVENUE

Amazingly enough, I graduated college with two degrees: one in advertising and one in sociology. I gave my saintly parents two for the price of one, since they were kind enough to support me through college.

After Syracuse, I went to work on Madison Avenue. That was my dream, to become an advertising executive. Like many kids, I had always wanted to be a baseball player, but that doesn't often happen in New York when you can only play three months a year. So, I figured if I couldn't play baseball for the Yankees, the next best thing for me was going to Madison Avenue and becoming an advertising executive.

By the time I got there, I'd been partying for four solid years, and I already knew that drugs were a problem for me. It was taking me longer and longer to recover – and more and more drugs to get the same high I used to get easily. I was still doing a lot of drugs, gambling and doing all the things that, by the world's standards, seemed fun, but it was becoming less fun and more of a noose around my neck. It finally got to the point where it was intolerable; I was in real trouble.

The first thing to give was the gambling. It had gotten to the point where even I realized I couldn't manage it anymore. I was going to get into real trouble. Either I was going to end up having my legs broken (or worse!) by some bookie I couldn't pay off, or I was going to lose everything I'd ever had.

I finally mustered up the courage to talk to my brother, Mike, who's four years older than me. He's a lawyer in New York City, and I remember saying to him, "Mike, I've got a gambling problem." Shocked, and not having a gambling problem himself, his first reaction was to say, "No, you don't."

I said, "No. You don't understand. I *do* have a gambling problem." He didn't realize how difficult this was for me to tell him. It was killing me to even say it. So I told him, honestly, "Not only that, but this is the only shot I have. I'm just telling you, if you don't help me, if you don't do something, I'm not asking anybody else again."

Mike said, "Okay, Boy." *Boy* was his little-brother nickname for me. "Okay, Boy. I'm going to help you. I'm going to find out where there's a Gambler's Anonymous meeting and I'm going to take you."

And he did. It was in New York City, and he took me to this place on 33rd Street, to this meeting, and took me to the door. Recognizing my fear, he asked, "Do you want me to come in with you?"

"No, no, no," I said, not entirely sure of myself. "I'll go in. But thanks."

I stayed in Gambler's Anonymous for a year. I'm telling you, it was the greatest thing I ever did. Week in, week out, I'd sit around a table with these guys who would share stories of what gambling had done to them in their lives – how it had ruined their lives, how they lost everything. I looked around that table. I was a 20-something young man. I looked at these 30-, 40-, 50-, 60-year old guys who had lost everything.

For one guy, it was sports betting. For another guy, it was the racetrack. For another guy, it was the casino. There was one particular guy who had a very unusual addiction. Remember, this was back in New York City in the early 80's. This guy's addiction was a pinball machine in a bar. If you played well, the bar gave you tickets, more credits for the pinball machine.

I'll never forget the look of pain on that guy's face – and I saw him week in, week out. I remember thinking to myself, "How could you possibly be addicted to a pinball machine in a bar?" I mean, I get why I bet sports – if I put up $1,000 and I win, I get another $1,000. That makes sense, right? I was a genius. But a pinball machine? How insane was that? I should have been answering my own question; I was just as insane as he was!

But I have news for you. His addiction, his pain, his suffering and his torment were exactly the same as mine. You see, addiction itself is the great equalizer. It's irrelevant *what* you're addicted to. It's the *addiction* that matters. It didn't matter that he was addicted to pinball and I was addicted to sports or the racetrack. The search for the thrill, and with it the ultimate pain it brought each one of us – that emotional emptiness, (that looking into the next bet for the next moment of time) was the same for everybody. That's what I came to realize in addiction.

This really isn't rocket science. This is the well-known nature of addiction. Whether it's the motorcycle guy doing 40 Percocet a day or me doing three a day, whether it's a guy doing 10 grams of coke a day, or another guy doing a gram, or whether one guy only parties on the weekends while the other guy parties every day... It doesn't matter. It's not the time of day you do it, or even the thing you're addicted to. It's the hold it has over your life. It's about what it causes you to think. It's how you obsess about it. It's about what you'll sacrifice to get it.

So, I realized that every single one of us in that room was in exactly the same spot. Addiction cuts across every demographic, psychographic, geographic line, every race, every color, every job occupation, every family. It doesn't matter where you came from, whom you are, where you were brought up, what you look like, what your job is. It matters that you suffer from this addiction and that pain of addiction is the same for everybody.

Sitting in that Gambler's Anonymous meeting with those guys was like *Scared Straight* for me. If you don't remember *Scared Straight*, or weren't old enough to see it back in the late 70's, it was a TV movie where they took young, first-time offenders, high school kids, and brought them into maximum security prisons with hardened criminals. The criminals were allowed to speak freely and tell the kids the real deal. Those guys – in prison for murder, rape, everything you can imagine – got up in the faces of these kids and told them exactly what prison life was like. They scared the living crap out of the high school kids who saw quite graphically where a criminal life would lead them. The kids were badly shaken afterward and were very determined not to wind up like those hardened criminals in jail. History would go on to show that most of the kids stayed straight after that life-changing experience.

I can tell you the same thing happened for me. I sat in that room with those Gambler's Anonymous guys, and I looked around at them and thought, "Man, that's me. That's my future. This is exactly where my life will wind up if I continue to gamble."

And I stopped.

But the problem for me was, I replaced one addiction with another. While I saw the outcome of the gambling, I didn't see the outcome of the drugs. I wasn't willing to give up drugs at that point.

So, I went to work on Madison Avenue. Drugs were still rampant in my life and getting progressively worse. At that point, I was what you might call a functioning drug addict. I loved my work and I was good at it, and I never did drugs during the day.

But nighttime, that was a different story. I'd come home at night and go *ballistic*. I would go through all the Quaaludes I could take. I'd get wasted to the point of no memory. Then I'd get up in the morning, go into work, and do my job. I functioned like this for years. I was taking Quaaludes, Xanax, Halcion; whatever I could get my hands on.

I don't know if you've ever taken Halcion, but it's the pill that your dentist uses so you'll forget what you felt in the dentist's chair. They call it "the little blue pill." At one point, at the height of my addiction, I was easily taking 24 to 30 Halcion a night.

Not only that, but I was going out and doing things at night of which I had no recollection. I drove to places and the only way I knew I had even gone out, or where I went, was I woke up the next morning to see shopping bags full of stuff in my apartment. I had absolutely no memory of going out and buying this stuff, but there it was!

I got calls from friends of mine: One went like this…

"Levine."

"Yeah?"

"You know you called me last night?"

"What? Oh, yeah. I know."

I'd lie, not wanting to get busted. But the truth is the next day I usually had no recollection of the people I had called the night before.

Another guy I often partied with knew I was messed up when I called him in the middle of the night. He called me the next afternoon and told me I called him at 2 AM and that we talked for an hour and had a perfectly normal conversation – but he knew I was messed up. The fact that it was 2 AM may have clued him in. The scary part was he told me that, if he didn't know me, he wouldn't have known how high I was because we were having a normal conversation. I didn't slur my words or anything. But I was wasted beyond belief and didn't remember one word of it the next day. That just shows you how much of a tolerance I had built up to drugs and how much of my life they had become.

I'm sure you've heard about people who testify in court cases about these drugs, where they say, "I murdered somebody and don't remember." *I get it.* You take too much Halcion, or mix it with Xanax – I get how you could do something serious and have no memory whatsoever the next day. It's a very, very dangerous drug.

It was finally cocaine that got the best of me. I was with Bozell and Jacobs Advertising in New York when I finally got to the point where I couldn't function. I'd been working on Madison Avenue for five years at that point, doing drugs through the entire period. I knew if I stayed in New York and continued to hang around the same people, I was going to die because there was no way for me to stop using drugs while hanging around the same people. I knew that the end was near. It wasn't a good situation.

I remember confessing to my father. Now my dad is an old school guy, and I don't think he really understood. I mean, he understood *English*. He knew what the *words* meant. My father had worked all his life and, when his own dad died, he took over the family business, and put my brother and me through college. He worked every day and didn't know anything about living a partying life. So, I knew he didn't fully comprehend what I was telling him.

I remember saying to him, "You know, Dad, I have a drug problem. And I think I'm going to move to Florida. I think I need a new start."

He looked at me and said, "Okay. Whatever you do, moving to Florida's great, but don't ever tell your mother why. Don't tell her you've got a drug problem." He wanted to protect her, which I understood.

In 1985 I moved to Florida. I quickly learned my next lesson- a lesson all addicts have to learn- you can't run from your problems because *you're* the problem. So, you know what? You take yourself, so your problem stays with you.

I read a great book called *How to Stop Worrying and Start Living* by Dale Carnegie. At the time in my life when I read it, I thought it was the greatest book ever. Today, I think it's the *second* greatest book ever (the *Bible* is the first), but it's still a great book. That book gave me the understanding that I couldn't run away from my problems. I couldn't run away from myself.

Some of the specifics might change, but at the root it's the same for every addict. We all go through the same process. The drug is just a symptom of the problem. If there's a fire burning in your house and you go and shut off the smoke alarm, you haven't put out the fire. The drugs (or the gambling, the alcohol, the sex, the food) are not the problem. They're a *symptom* of the problem. Your disease, your *addiction*, is the problem.

I drove from New York to Florida with my dog and all my worldly possessions in the car, doing Valium the whole way down. Don't ask me how we made it, but we did. The first thing I did when I arrived was to find an old high school buddy of mine, who had also moved down, who could hook me up with cocaine. He got me some, so I dove right back into cocaine.

I also had, at that time, a girlfriend from the advertising agency in New York, whom I had just started seeing about a month before the move. She decided to move down, and move in with me.

I had a wonderful aunt who gave me a job as her advertising director in a national stock brokerage company located in Boca Raton, Florida. I think my aunt knew what was going on with me, but she also sort of *didn't* want to know. So, she just tried to help me however she could. It seemed like everything was coming together, but really it was just coming further apart.

My girlfriend and I partied our brains out. We did drugs together – it was part of our thing – but it finally got so bad that even she couldn't take it anymore. And she left me.

Needless to say, I was distraught. I moved down to Florida for a fresh start and instead, I was still addicted. I did not overcome anything and my girlfriend dumped me. I had hit many lows before, but that was the lowest up to that point. I didn't know what to do.

Occasionally, when I lived in New York, I would stop in St. Patrick's Cathedral on my walk from the subway to work, usually just to get out of the bitter cold of a New York winter. I'd sit in there and pray, just liking the peace and serenity of the church, and the fact that nobody bothered me.

I was looking for that same feeling when I went into the door of a church in Florida one Tuesday in 1991. I wasn't a religious guy, but I was at the end of my rope. I went in to pray and just laid it all out to God. I remember saying, "God, I can't stop this on my own. I need help. I'm in a bad spot." Something amazing, something absolutely life-changing happened to me. God spoke to me that day, in my heart, and He made me realize that I needed to put my trust and faith in Him. I started a journey of faith that day, as I gradually – very gradually – began to trust God. I say "very gradually" because I have to tell you, even though God changed my life that day and I started to put my faith and trust in Him, I didn't give up drugs right away. In fact, I didn't give them up for years. But God started to work in areas of my life, gradually.

I'm not saying that you'll have the same experiences, and I'm not saying that it's a requirement that you do. But that's my experience and I want you to know it, so you can benefit from it and hopefully not make the same mistakes I made, or put yourself through the pain and suffering I brought upon myself and others. It may sound cliché, but I assure you it's true... The desire of my heart is that if I can help even one person live a better life and not go through the crap, pain and torture I suffered from my battle with addiction, then this book, and everything I went through, will have been worth it.

7
MARRIAGE

Though I was still an addict, things began to go very well for me in business. In Florida, a partner and I began a television production company that grew by leaps and bounds, growing to over 200 employees.

Not long after my girlfriend left me, having had enough of me and my addiction, I met a nice girl in Florida and we got married. After my experience at the church in 1991, where I believe I personally encountered God, I gradually became more spiritual and started to look for God's help and answers in all things. My new wife was starting to become uncomfortable with my spiritual pursuits. But a much bigger problem was the fact that I was still using drugs, and she knew it.

Marriage can be difficult even when both spouses are healthy and functioning well; in our case, I was a mess, and it didn't provide much of a foundation on which to build a young marriage.

Let me tell you something. This is a critical insight into addict behavior. She would always ask me, "What's wrong? How can I help you? You can talk to me. We're married." But I never told her a *thing*. I loved her. She was so sweet and understanding. But I never told her the truth about how I felt, about what was going on in my life, about what was important, about what things I was doing, about what I thought in my inner self. I just couldn't bring myself to do it. I had an image of myself that I wanted her, and the whole world, to have; and that's what I tried to project to her, rather than let her into my struggle. I just needed her to have this image of me, which is, of course, ridiculous – but that's the way addiction works.

The addict is in denial and won't admit his problems, but you can see it. Often, the whole world can see it.

So, there was this poor, sweet girl who only wanted to do what she was supposed to do as a wife. She wanted to love her husband, help her husband, be closer to her husband and I was unable to give her that emotional intimacy and closeness. That's another trait of a drug addict: the inability to share those intimate thoughts because of feelings of low self-esteem, low self-value, low worth.

The final straw that ended our marriage was my going on a cocaine binge one day. When I finally came home, I remember she was extremely upset. She'd finally had enough. I remember lying on the floor in a haze and, as she walked out, she screamed at me that I was a loser and would always be a loser. She slammed the door.

We got divorced.

8

EDDIE

My partner for nine years in the TV Production business, Mark, was not a drug user at all. Occasionally, he'd have a Captain Morgan, but that was the extent of his drug use. Of course, I could recognize the employees who were drug users so, if I realized they had a problem, we sent them to rehab – all the while still having a drug problem of my own.

One day, Mark shared with me that his brother-in-law from Buffalo had a severe drug problem that was ruining his life. His wife was fed up, and getting ready to divorce him. My partner asked me if there was anything we could do. Not being a drug guy himself, he didn't know what to do.

I said, "Look, fly him down. Tell him we have a potential job for him – because the only way he's going to come down is if there's some excuse. Let me talk to him."

So we brought Mark's brother-in-law, Eddie, down, and I took him to the track. I had a couple of Jack Daniels' with him, and we started to develop a rapport. Finally, I asked him what was going on in his life – what was the problem.

Pausing to think, he opened up to me.

"You know, I have a problem," he said.

Looking him in the eye, I asked him the most important question I could ask him. "Do you want help?"

With sudden firmness, he agreed he did. We decided right then and there that he would go into rehab.

Eddie said to me later – he would tell me the story he would also tell people when he spoke to AA (Alcoholics Anonymous) groups, and NA (Narcotics Anonymous) groups, and in prisons – "You were the only person in my life who ever asked me if I wanted help."

Remember that. It's not enough to acknowledge that you've got a drug problem. The question is: do you want help? Because *if you want help, there is help* – and this is the great news for all addicts... And their parents... And their spouses... And their children. If you want help, there is help. There is a way out. God says in the *Bible*:

No temptation has overtaken you that is not common to man. God is faithful, and he will not let you be tempted beyond your ability, but with the temptation he will also provide the way of escape, that you may be able to endure it. (1 Corinthians 10:13)

Eddie said, "Yes, I want help," so we put him through drug rehab. He came out as a model for recovery. God did so much with this guy's life; it was a *miracle* what happened. He was a *model*. He got right with his higher power, for Eddie that was Jesus Christ, and went on to live a wonderful life of recovery, talking and telling people all about how to get better, and sharing his own story.

Now, as I mentioned, at the time he came down from Buffalo to see me, Eddie was in the process of getting divorced; his wife was in the final stages of filing divorce papers. When he said he was going into rehab, his wife called me and asked, "What should I do? Should I not divorce him?"

I said, "You need to continue on exactly as you're planning to do. File the papers. Go through with it, because I can't promise you that there's going to be any change in his life. I can't promise you anything, except we'll see what happens.

If I were you, I would follow through and do what you need to do."

She did divorce him.

And guess what? They wound up getting back together after his recovery. He regained his wife and his kids, and they lived happily for nine years after that until he unfortunately died of a heart attack in his 40's. Yet he packed more living and giving into those nine years than most people pack into an entire lifetime. What God did in those nine years with Eddie's surrendered life, with his *recovered* life was amazing. Eddie reached and helped thousands of people! You can't even believe all the people he touched. At his funeral, there were hundreds of people from all over, from every walk of life. From prisons to flea markets, he touched people everywhere he went.

But even as I helped him into recovery, I still was battling my own drug problem. After he went through rehab, he came back into my office. Eddie said to me words that utterly haunted me. He said, "Rehab was incredible. It saved my life. I learned *why* I did drugs."

Those words cut through me like a knife. I realized, "Wow. I don't know why *I* do drugs." Oh, I knew why I *told* myself I did them. It was because I liked the high, or I just wanted to, or whatever. But in reality, I realized I didn't really know *why* I did drugs. I found myself really jealous that he knew why *he* did drugs and I couldn't answer the question of why *I* did.

My drug use continued. Our business was taking off. My partner Mark and I were working hard; but I was still partying and doing cocaine. Mark, though he wasn't a drug guy, got wind that something was going on with me, and he didn't like it. It's hard to run a successful business when your business partner (me!) was disappearing occasionally for days at a time.

9
BREAKTHROUGH

One day in 1996, I'll never forget, I had missed work for a couple of days and there was a pounding on my door. It was Mark. I was lying there naked - which is not that unusual when you're doing cocaine - and I could barely even talk. I was fried. My throat was dry, and I was in a daze. He probably heard the words, "Go away!" out of my mouth, at most.

And he said, through the door, "I'm not going away. And if you don't open the door, I'm calling the cops."

Now that was an interesting proposition. You don't want the cops. Believe me, you don't want the cops. So, I dragged myself up, put some pants on, and opened the door. He came in and we talked. God bless him; he was very, very sympathetic. I thought he was going to read me the riot act, but he didn't.

He said, "Look, I love you. You have a problem. I want to get you help. Let's talk about that."

So, there it was, my problem exposed and out in the open. But I was reluctant, as I hadn't really hit bottom... YET!! I wasn't ready to give up using. I agreed with Mark I needed help, but I convinced him (I was lying...big surprise!) I would get my act together on my own and put an end to my destructive behavior. Yet, it was incredibly difficult. I was determined to stop, but I couldn't. I'd start with good intentions, and then end up completely wasted again.

Not long after, I was on a vacation with a bunch of friends in Lake Tahoe. Lying in my bed there, it hit me with full force: "I can't stop on my own." Right then and there, I spoke to God.

"God? You have to help me. I can't do this on my own. You have to help me."

A week later, I came home from Lake Tahoe, and I was driving. It was 10 o'clock at night, I was taking pills and drinking alcohol, and I completely blacked out behind the wheel. I crashed through a fence and wound up about 15 feet from a lake.

The jolt from the crash – and the exploding airbag – woke me up from my stupor. I got out of the car, wearing only swim trunks, a t-shirt and no shoes. I started walking around the car; it was almost pitch black out. There were no lights anywhere. I couldn't get the car going again, but I was so wasted, I didn't even know I'd had an accident. I thought the car had stalled! One thing I knew was nobody was going to find me there, so I had to find my way back to civilization. I had a gun in the glove compartment (I had a concealed weapons permit), which I pulled out and stuffed into my swim trunks in case I needed protection.

I had crashed in an area where they were in the midst of building a new county park, so there were woods, a lake, and couple of bulldozers. In true addict fashion, I decided to climb into one of the bulldozers to see if it would start, with the idea that I could drive back out of the park on it, but there was no key. Gee what a surprise!

Still trying to find my way out, my next move was to climb down a steep set of rocks, wade through the lake, and climb back up another set of rocks on the other side of the lake. I made it – scraped and bloody – and was wandering around the park, completely lost.

The next thing I knew, it was daybreak. I'd wandered all night. In the breaking light, I could see a construction trailer. I'd been wandering around so long, and I was so confused from the drugs and the wreck, that I thought the car, which I couldn't find anymore, had now been stolen.

I found a guy at the construction trailer, and I said, "Hey, somebody stole my car. Can I use your phone?" I have no idea what they must've made of me at that moment, but taking pity on me, they gave me the phone. I called my business partner Mark, but got no answer. I then called his wife. Thankfully, she answered.

"Hey, my car stalled on me. Then, the craziest thing is, somebody stole it. Come get me!" She said, "Okay. I'll be right there."

When Mark's wife got there, she asked me what happened. I told her we had to go look for the car. I got in with her, and she drove me around the park, looking for it. I said, "Isn't this amazing? Somebody stole my car, after it stalled! I went looking for help after it stalled, and somebody stole the car." (Hey, it made sense to *me*.)

Still not having found the car, she took me back to my house and I called the police to report my car stolen. They said they'd be right over.

The police arrived in just a few moments – and they were furious.

"I don't understand. What's the problem? Why are you angry?" I asked, not having a clue.

"We found your car. We know where your car is, and we know you were driving it, wrecked it, and then left it."

"No!" I protested. "All I know is the car stalled, and I got out to go for help, and somebody stole the car. Why would I call you guys if I did that?" I was telling the truth – as far as I knew it. I really believed what I was saying, even though it was clearly ridiculous.

The cop looked at me, and he was *pissed*. He said, "All I know is you're a businessman, and you got some motivation for doing this. I don't know what it is, but you got some motivation for doing this." He knew that my story was nonsense, and he was sure I was up to something. Yet I believed my own insanity!

Of course, they found the car and towed it. It was totally destroyed. I had plowed through a heavy fence after making a right turn instead of a left turn to my house. I never saw the fence, and almost drove into the lake. In my condition, I could have easily drowned and it could have all been over that night.

I knew that was the end. I knew that I had to go to rehab in a serious way. The jig was up, and I was busted. It was the best thing that ever happened to me. Finally. I had *hit bottom* and really wanted help!

I went to a rehab center and I sat down to talk with a counselor. I knew I needed help, but I also knew I didn't want to live in a rehabilitation facility for four weeks. I was still terrified at the idea of going into rehab, even though I knew I needed help.

So, in true addict style, I offered the counselor a deal: I would go to rehab for 28 days, but they'd have to let me go home at 8pm every evening to sleep at my own house. The rehab center owner rightly refused my deal, but he did tell me something that was extremely important to me. He said to me, "Listen, I'd have a lot of respect for you if you climb up to the top of the mountain, look down, and tell me you don't like what you see. But I'll have no respect for you if you won't go up and even take a look." It was like he was challenging me, saying, "I dare you to go look and see." I had nothing to lose.

People often do that when telling others about God, too. I've done it myself. They'll say, "Go search God and see if He's there. If He says He'll show up and doesn't, you can come back and tell me He's a liar. But don't tell me you didn't even look." That's just lame.

I share that with every addict I talk to today. What ultimately allowed me go into rehab was this knowledge: I could keep using drugs if I wanted. I wasn't signing a contract. I wasn't making a lifetime commitment to anybody. That mentality gave me the courage and freedom to say, "You know what? I've got to check this out. I've got to know if they're liars or not." I jumped into it always knowing in my own head (and even knowing to this day) I can do drugs anytime I want. Nobody's telling me what to do, what I can and can't do. It's *my* choice, what I do and how I want to live. Understanding that was *my* key.

As I mentioned, however, the rehab center was not willing to let me go home in the evenings, so I tracked down another counselor who would go along with my idea.

The first morning, I went to the counselor's house, and within a half-hour, I was looking at him like he was a psychic. I mean, it was *eerie*. After knowing me for only 30 minutes, he was telling me all these things about myself and my life with an accuracy that I couldn't believe.

"How could you possibly know all these things about me?" I asked him in wonderment. He looked at me and he laughed.

"All addicts are basically the same," he said. "You are an addict so you have the traits of an addict."

I didn't understand what those were. "What do you mean, *the traits of an addict*?" The counselor, a recovering addict himself, started to educate me about addiction. 28 days later, I finally knew what my friend Eddie had meant when he said, "I know why I do drugs."

I understood. I saw the mindset. I saw how an addicts brain works. I saw that was *my* brain. I saw the choices I had going forward. The struggle was nowhere near over, but now I had the knowledge and information, and a new determination to stop.

That was the turning point that saved my life.

10
UNDERSTANDING

I remember distinctly feeling as if I was being pulled down into a pit, into a fiery pit, by the drugs. This wasn't just a one second flash or a dream. It was a growing feeling that took root and expanded day by day. I remember feeling like Satan had grabbed onto my leg, and was pulling me down into a fiery pit. I could feel myself slipping away.

For many, many years during my drug use, I remember thinking very clearly that I could always come back. What happened was I'd party, I'd cross over the line, but I was always able to get back. In college, I could recover in a day. As I got older, it took longer. It would take three days or a week to recover. But I had *always* felt that no matter how far over the line I went, I could always bring myself back. I was able to do that – until this time. The car accident was when I knew I couldn't bring myself back anymore.

It was the single scariest moment in my life. Not the accident itself, but the full realization of what I had become. I thought I was in control. I wasn't in control. The drugs were in control and there was no way back. The pit of Hell had me; the drugs had me.

It was a horrible, awful realization. I know that if *you're* suffering from any kind of addiction, the pleasure from that addiction has long since disappeared. Undoubtedly, it was there in the beginning. Whether it's drugs, alcohol, pornography, gambling, eating, shopping, the Internet, work – whatever the addiction of choice is, I know that the pleasure you got from it is long, long gone.

Most non-addicts wonder why the addict continues to do these things that are so un-pleasurable and destructive. They wonder why a guy would gamble his family's rent and food money away? Why would someone risk her job, her health, her sanity on drugs and alcohol? Why would a guy stay on the Internet looking at pornography, when he's got a wife who wants to love him? Or kids who want to play with him and hug him and who need their daddy? Why?

In rehabilitation, one of the counselors answered that question in a powerful way that has stuck with me. He said, "There's comfort in familiar pain."

Maybe you've seen the movie *The Shawshank Redemption*. In that movie, these guys are stuck in an awful prison with corrupt wardens and guards. Yet when one of them would be released after years in the prison, he'd often immediately commit another crime to try to get sent back. Why? The outside world was unfamiliar and frightening. The inside of the prison, though painful, was *comforting* to them. Though a kind of hell on earth, it had become home "There's comfort in familiar pain." That, to a large degree, is addiction in a nut- shell. We go to a place that's familiar.

Let me tell you something about my drug addiction and my gambling addiction. As I told you, I love to gamble. I love to do drugs. I hated the *downside* of it. I hated the pain of losing when I gambled. I hated the coming down with drugs. But when I did drugs and gambled, I was in a place where you couldn't touch me. I was in control of the world. I was in my own world where I was the king; I was the boss. I did whatever I wanted, when I wanted. There was a tremendous feeling of power that came with that. It was a tremendous feeling of freedom – even though it was actually an illusion.

The thing offering the feeling of freedom wound up being a prison.

But there is hope of escape. Earlier, I mentioned one of my favorite Bible verses. This is a promise from God.

> *"...God is faithful; he will not let you be tempted beyond what you can bear. But when you are tempted, he will also provide a way out so that you can endure it...." (1 Corinthians 10:13)*

After God says there's no temptation that overtakes you except what's common to man, the next line is, "but with the temptation He will also provide the way of escape." I'm here to tell you: whether you're an addict yourself, or a parent or spouse of an addict, there is a way out. The only question is: will you take it or not? There is help if you want help. I'll have much more to say about that in Part III of this book.

But I'm here to tell you that it's been almost 20 years since I took the way of escape, and my life has gotten better every day since then. I know who I am, what I am, why I am.

My turnaround began during that night in Lake Tahoe when I asked God for help. Let me tell you a follow-up story. Ten years later I was back in Lake Tahoe, on vacation with an entirely new group of friends. We had all gone out to a restaurant, and we were lingering over a wonderful dinner. The conversation was bright and engaging in a way I seldom experienced during my drug days. As we were all sitting at the table, I was telling one of the stories I shared earlier with you about something my drug-dealing friends and I did back in college.

My friend's wife Yvette, a wonderfully sweet woman, looked at me, stunned. "Why Jack Levine," she exclaimed, "I would have never imagined *you* would ever do something like that!"

My reaction might surprise you. I went back up to my hotel room that night and I *cried*. Tears of joy! The story I'd told about college really *was* me – back then. Through my tears, I said, "God, thank you so much for what you've done in my life, that when people look at me today, they don't think of me as a drug addict wasting his life. As a matter of fact, it's so far removed from what I am now that people can't even believe that *would've* been me. Thank you for making that *unbelievable* change in me. Thank you that, today, I'm a new person. You've truly given me a new life."

PART II
RICKY'S STORY

11
A WIFE AND A SON

As I told you, a couple of years after my first wife left me, I finally got clean and sober. I waited six years for my second wife. When I say *waited*, I mean that I was determined to wait on God to provide the right woman for me. And God is faithful; He did bless me with a wonderful woman, Beth, whom I married in 2000. Her son, Ricky, was 11 years old when we got married. His father, Beth's first husband, had died when Ricky was just a baby.

Now, Beth is a recovering alcoholic and drug addict. When we married, she hadn't had a drink or drug in more than 15 years. I think it was helpful to our relationship that she too understood the nature of addiction. With my first wife, I was incapable of intimately sharing who I was, including my experiences and feelings. But having gone through rehabilitation and counseling, I'd learned who and what I was, and I didn't have the fear of sharing the "real me" anymore.

So with Beth, I was honest almost to a fault. I made very clear up front exactly what she was getting. I told her that I was a recovering drug addict and recovering gambling addict, and that for better or for worse, warts and all, this is who she was getting.

I'm a big Bob Dylan fan, and Dylan has always been known to be hard to interpret. He was so mysterious that people used to rummage through his garbage to try to find out more about who he was and what he was thinking. He did a song called "Covenant Woman" where he sang about his wife knowing him so well that there were no hidden, secret things. That's the way I am now with Beth, which is a massive change from my previous life.

Beth's son Ricky and I bonded from the very start. It was the most natural thing in the world. He'd had no father growing up and immediately gravitated to me as his father, and I immediately bonded with him as my son. Sometimes in blended families, there can be friction between the children and the new spouse, but we are very fortunate. There is no hint of that with us. It is just wonderful. I legally adopted Ricky as soon as Beth and I got married, and though Beth and I have since had the blessing of two more wonderful children, Jackson and Talia, I make no distinction between my relationships with the three of them. They are each equally and absolutely my child.

Ricky and I shared a number of passions together, including sports and music. As he went through middle and high school, his musical interest increased, and he began to develop into an incredibly talented saxophone player. He took lessons and played in the band at school.

My relationship with him remained strong, and I poured into him as his father, teaching him about life and God and everything I believed was ultimately important. At the same time, Ricky was into bodybuilding, which included a ton of work in the weight room and a carefully controlled diet.

He understood his mother's history because we would talk about it a lot. We never hid any of our issues from him, and instead used them as points of teaching and guidance. We talked about the fact – and Ricky understood clearly through those talks – that given his genetic make-up, he has a predisposition to addiction (as opposed to someone without the same make-up). Also, there was a good chance if he were to ever pick up a drink or drug, he would become an addict.

"Oh no, I'd never put a drug in my mouth. My body is my temple – it's pure," he told me when he was 16.

12
THE FALL

After he graduated from high school, he was accepted into Berklee College of Music in Boston, Massachusetts. It's the number one school for modern music in the country. Though my business had done well, Berklee cost a ton of money. We were willing to make the sacrifice because God had so clearly gifted Ricky with this amazing talent to play the saxophone, and as his parents we wanted to do whatever we could to nurture and encourage him to pursue his passion and talents. We wanted him to have the best life possible, and we believed that studying under some of the greatest music teachers in the world would help him toward that goal.

Now, you have to understand something about us. On Ricky's cell phone when he was in high school, I'm listed under "CIA." We were not absentee, uninvolved parents. I knew Ricky, knew what he was up to, who he was hanging out with, and generally what he was doing at any given moment. But even so, there's only so much you can do when you are 1,300 miles away.

So, we dropped Ricky off at the Berklee College of Music in Boston. Almost immediately upon arrival, he began to party his brains out, drinking a lot and doing drugs. I caught on pretty quickly to what was happening because, as I told you, I'm "CIA" with him, and having been through all the partying and addictive behaviors myself, I can smell it in an instant. Needless to say, it was heartbreaking. Nobody wants their child to throw away his life and, having been in the pit of despair, both Beth and I knew even more than many about the potential heartbreak that lay ahead.

In short order, Ricky began to fail miserably at Berklee. I would talk to him about it, but I didn't think I was getting through to him, so I would also write him these long letters. (You know: *Son, this is a mistake and let me tell you what I learned and don't do this and don't throw away your future and don't be foolish*.) I love writing letters, by the way, because the recipient can't talk back to you. I've heard some great testimonies where people say that somebody had written them a letter that deeply impacted them. They kept the letter and read it over and over again. So I knew there was power in writing letters, and I poured out myself in these heartfelt pleas to Ricky.

But it wasn't working. I went up there to visit him and try to talk to him in person about the road he was headed down. He'd listen, but still nothing changed.

I'd get calls in the middle of the night... Once when he was in the emergency room after he put his hand through a wall. Drunk calls. You know those kind of calls: "Blah, Blah, I love you... I'm so sorry... I'm an idiot... I'm throwing my life away... I can't believe I'm doing this and I'm such a screw up... I won't do this again... Blah, blah, blah." This became commonplace.

For him, going to college was an explosion of freedom. He had this opportunity for the first time to do whatever he wanted. Obviously, his ideas had changed about bodybuilding and the purity of his body – he was increasingly willing to put more and more unnatural stuff in there, including drugs. My mother and father had given him an old Toyota, which he cracked it up in a drunk-driving accident. He was on a roll.

Unsurprisingly, he flunked out of Berklee after the year. He moved back home, and I began to sit down regularly to have "the talk" with him, telling him that I loved him and wanted what was best for him. Berklee had been a washout.

"Let's chalk this one up to experience," I told him. I got him a counselor to talk to, but that didn't work. He manipulated the guy. He just wasn't ready to give up his drug use.

I remember asking him, "Why are you doing this now?"

He said, "I would have done it a lot earlier in high school, but I knew there was no way I could have gotten away with it with you guys."

After returning home, things didn't get better with Ricky; they got worse. I pulled a favor with a friend of ours who had a connection at Florida International University in Miami - a good school with a good music program. I told Ricky, "Okay, it's not Berklee, but it's a good school. You have a second chance there."

So Ricky Went to FIU in Miami. Same thing. Failed all the classes – every one. Flunked out in a year. He was spending all his time partying, and had become a raging drunk and drug addict. I mean, *raging*. He had blackouts on a regular basis. I made at least three trips to the emergency room to pick him up. Beth and I were terrified because, as recovering addicts ourselves, we knew what was going on. We just *knew* that the phone was going to ring in the middle of the night. I'd be the one who answered the phone, and I'd be the one who went to the emergency room. I'd be the one to take the pictures – this car accident, that car accident... all the car accidents.

It felt like all our lives were spiraling out of control. I'd say, "Rick, you're blowing it. This doesn't make sense. This is crazy!" And he'd just look at me.

I said, "Do you want help?"

"No, I don't want help."

He was stealing from us too, at that point. Now, remember, Beth and I have two other kids, who were young. Jackson was six and Talia was four at the time. Beth and I talked intensely, and I said, "Honey, you have to make this decision. You know there's no difference in my love for Ricky than my biological children because I just love them so much, but something awful could end up happening, and if it does, we can't blame each other for it. What do you want to do?"

We agreed, "He's not living in our house anymore. This is what we have to do." We both realized that we could very possibly get a call one night that he was in jail - or in the morgue - because I can tell you he was a dead man walking. He had no shot at that point. He didn't want help.

13
CHOICES

After offering Ricky as much help as I knew how to offer, and having him refuse it, I had to have one of the most difficult talks I've ever had with anyone in my life.

Looking him square in the eye, I said, "Listen, son. I want you to be really clear about this. I love you and we love you. But you can't live here anymore. I can't take a chance with who your friends are. We've got little kids here."

So Ricky became virtually homeless.

He got fired from a restaurant management job and several other places for stealing to support his growing, deadly habits. I remember saying to him, "Listen, son, you have no shot. I'm a gambler. If there was even a 99-to-1 shot, if you were the highest odds on the board but there was still even a *chance* that you could possibly win, I'd say, "Well, there's a chance, but I'm telling you that you have no shot. You're a lock to lose" (A "lock" is a gambling term meaning "a sure thing.") "I'd bet everything I have against you. Everything. Not because I don't love you – I *do* love you. But I'm telling you what I see and what I know. On your current course, you are going to wind up dead or in jail."

I remember, one time, this kid – one of his deadbeat friends – dropped him off when he came over for dinner or something, and Ricky needed to give him gas money. Of course, Ricky didn't have any money to give him.

I said, "Rick, go on into the house. I'll give the kid the money."

I went over to the kid's car. I gave him $20. I said, "Thanks for bringing Ricky home. Now, I just want to tell you, *you're killing him."* I got in the kid's face and I *screamed.* I said, "I just want you to know, if you enable him and he dies, it's on *you."* I remembered one of my old drug buddies in college getting screamed at by the manager of Lowell George, lead singer from the band Little Feat. My friend had sold him cocaine, and George died of an overdose. The manager had screamed at my friend, "You killed him by selling him all that cocaine!" It was an extremely effective and memorable moment, so I figured, alright, I'm going that route, too.

"If anything happens to Ricky," I added for good measure to drive the point home, "I'm going to hunt you down and kill you."

That sounds extreme, and it is. But like any desperate, loving parent, I was terrified about what was happening to Ricky, and I would have tried anything at that point to save him. Intimidation, love, threats, whatever. Threatening his friend who was enabling him was not an issue for me. What did I have to lose? I was a desperate parent.

The kid left. Ricky was in the house, and I told him the absolute, immediate danger I believed he was in. I said, "Ricky, you're near the end here. You're going to wind up in the morgue or in jail. There's no other option. I want to help you. There's help, but you've got to choose it."

He looked me straight in the eye and he said the most chilling words I have ever heard anybody say.

"I don't want it," he said flatly. "I'm choosing to live this life."

I'm telling you, those were the most terrifying words I ever heard in my life.

Beth and I knew there was nothing we could do but pray. We had no control. Believe it or not, I actually thought of having him *kidnapped*. That's how desperate we were. I have a buddy who is a former bounty hunter, and he said, "Listen. We'll grab him. We'll throw him in the car. Before he knows what happened, he'll be in the field in Montana at this camp, he'll stay there for a year and hopefully they'll clean him up."

I'm telling you, it was in my mind, a *legitimate option*. I wrestled with it. I prayed about it. I justified it, saying, "God, I need to save his life. This is the right thing to do!" And then I thought about how I would have felt if someone had done that to me in my own addiction. In addition to being scary and barbaric, it wouldn't have worked. I knew it had to be his choice, win, lose, or draw.

When Ricky told us those chilling words – "I'm choosing this life" – we had already made the decision that we were going to be tough with him. Now, I hasten to say – and this was critical – we didn't cut him out of our lives. I always said to him, "Son, I love you. I want to hang out with you. We're not cutting you out of our life. But, I'm not enabling your lifestyle. I'm not paying for it, and you're not going to do it around your little brother and sister. You're not going to expose us to it; but I love you no matter what, and I want to be a part of your life."

The textbook will tell you to cut someone off in this situation and stop enabling him, which we were able to do with love and understanding. We were lucky. Ricky seemed to understand. When we told him we were cutting him off (without cutting him *out*), he didn't say, "Oh, screw you. You're cutting me off, so I'll never talk to you again." He very well could have said that – and many addicts do. You need to be prepared for that response if that's the step you take with an addict in your life. It's the right step, but there are no guaranteed results. When you love someone, you're willing to do what's best for them even if they hate it – or hate *you* for it.

When I counsel parents now, I'll tell them, "Listen. Clearly, you're enabling your child, and this is not good for their recovery. But I also want to tell you something: Beth and I cut our son off, leaving him homeless. We had prepared ourselves for the very real possibility of a call from the morgue or the jail. If you're not prepared for that call, then don't cut him off, because you're taking the ultimate risk. Otherwise, you can choose to keep enabling him and you'll have a drug-addicted son, but at least you will know where he is and see him all the time." For some parents, that is a trade they are willing to make, although tragically one that never leads to the addict's recovery.

I have one friend who hasn't been able to do it. He has a son in his 40's who's by all appearances a hopeless alcoholic and drug addict. My friend fears that if he cut his son off, he'll lose him forever. I understand that. But I also know he can lose him anyway if his son doesn't stop using drugs. These are among the torturous choices that loved ones of addicts have to make.

14
CRISIS

Things were getting bad for Ricky. He had a lot of speeding tickets from all his drug abuse, and he'd frequently spent a few days in jail here and there. For instance, one night in a blackout, he took a shopping cart and put it through a shoe store window. He pulled shoes out of the window as the alarm was going off and put them in the back of his car. Then he took the shopping cart and broke *another* window, into the deli next door. Why? To get a soda out of the soda machine. The cops came to arrest him. And because he had a knife from the deli in his hand, he was arrested for *armed burglary*. What can I say... When it rains it pours.

Another night, he was out driving around messed up and had another accident. He completely totaled the car. Thankfully, once again, his injuries were not life threatening. I went to get him at the emergency room, and I could see it all over his face – he was *wasted*. He had a hole in his arm from the accident, about the size of a baseball, but he could hardly feel it because he was so hammered. I even took pictures of him on my cell phone so that I could show him what he looked like once he sobered up.

Things got to a critical point with Ricky. I could see the end in sight, and it wasn't a good one.

"You're not even going to make it 30 days, Son," I told him, hoping to open his eyes.

Eight days later, he flipped over his car on I-95 at 2 o'clock in the morning. In the middle of the night, we got a call from the emergency room at Boca Raton Community Hospital. "Sir, your son's been in an accident." I held my breath.

Miraculously, though he'd flipped his car, he made it through with only a few minor injuries. And, unbelievably enough, the police didn't charge him with anything. (Either they didn't want to hassle with the paperwork in the middle of the night or God's hand was on him). It was 6 or 7 o'clock in the morning when I brought him home. Then I let him sleep it off – which he did for about a day and a half.

Finally, he woke up and had his senses about him. I sat down with him and said, "Buddy, I'm not mad at you. Now listen, here are your choices." He seemed more attentive to what I was saying than usual. Normally, he blew me off when we started to have this talk. I said, "You can leave if you want. No harm, no foul. You were in the emergency room and I came and bailed you out again. I let you sleep it off. You know, I love you and I wish you were living differently."

I let it sink in for a minute. "Or, there's help if you want it."

For the first time, rather than blowing me off, he said, "Can I think about it?"

"You have the rest of the day," I said.

At the end of the day, he came back to me. "Yeah," he said. "I want help." (I think he was scared about how accurate my predictions about him were, in terms of timing and reality.) It was the greatest thing I ever heard. I arranged for Ricky to go right into rehab.

As is sometimes the case, however, it didn't take the first time. After he got out, he returned quickly to his drinking and drugging.

15
NEW LIFE

Then he did something stupid. He got caught with drugs, and was arrested and sentenced to 30 days in jail. Though he'd had car accidents, trips to the ER, and spent the odd night in jail, this was going to be his first extended stay in the slammer.

I took him to the jail the day he had to surrender himself and begin his 30-day sentence. You know how, in the movies, you see the door shut and you hear the clank? That's exactly what it was. I watched my son get taken away, and the jail door rolled shut and clanked on his life.

The 30 days in jail were a godsend. When he came out, he was no longer such a tough guy. The time behind bars had convinced him he really wanted to do whatever he needed to do to turn his life around. It never mattered how much Beth and I wanted it for him; we couldn't make him do it. Nobody could make *me* do it, and I can't make *you* do it, and you can't make your addict spouse or child do it. The best we can do is to show them what their options are and that there is help.

So, today, there's a happy ending to the story. Ricky, who looked me in the eye and said, "I'm choosing to live this life" of drugs and alcohol has now chosen to live another life. He's been clean and sober for over two years, as of this writing. He works in the drug rehabilitation field helping other addicts. I've told you his story with Ricky's complete permission.

This kid, who was lost, who was a dead man walking, now has a purpose and passion and direction for his life unlike everything I've ever seen before. As his father, it's just amazing to me – his healthy mindset, his humility, and his appreciation for life. It's not about material things with him. It's just

about the gift of being *alive*. He realizes that life *is* a present –
to be *lived* in the present. It's not to be lived buried in the
past with guilt, and it's not to be lived in agony over what the
future might hold. It's to be lived in the present.

Ricky's taken responsibility for all the things he's done in
the past. He's made amends where he can, and has followed
the Alcoholics Anonymous recovery program in such a great
and wonderful way. He amazes me with the man he's grown
into, and he's such a gift from God to me and to Beth. I can't
tell you how proud I am of him.

Is there a part of me that thinks there was another path for
him? Yes – and I know what that other path was. That other
path for him was to the grave. He might have been a great sax
player for a year or two; I have no doubt he would've been
successful because of his talent. I had great connections for
him in the music industry, and there were lots of possibilities
open to him. But I now know he never would have survived.

A couple of months ago, we were driving together. He
turned to me and said, "Dad, you know, by the world's standards, I'm a total failure."

I looked back at him. Of course, I'm his dad, and that's not
what I want to hear him say. "No, Son," I protested. "Don't be
ridiculous."

He said, "No, Dad. Here's the thing. If you look at the
world's standards, I've flunked out of college, I have no car, I
was homeless, and I have no money. I lost everything I had. I
had this great opportunity to go into music, and I blew that.
I've been to jail. I make $11 an hour. I'm 24 years old. By the
world's standards, I'm a failure."

He let it sink in a second.

"But I have never been happier or more satisfied in all of my life."

Ricky realized something that many people don't realize in a lifetime. Most of that stuff doesn't matter. He now possesses what makes for a real *life*: peace, happiness, self-worth, self-esteem, a driving purpose. That's the greatest gift he could ever have. His future is very bright and more importantly HE HAS A FUTURE! The funniest part of all is I believe he will wind up making a lot of money and be very successful professionally – just not in music. I'm sure God has other plans... Better plans... God always does!

Many times, Beth and I will talk to friends who are having similar problems with their kids. They ask us, "How did you do it? How did you cut off your kid?"

I tell them, "It wasn't a question of *how*. There was no other option. He was a dead man walking. There was absolutely no other option. So, as a parent, I can sympathize with the pain you're going through. I can sympathize with the lack of control that you're feeling. I can sympathize with the frustration that you have."

I tell them that I know exactly how they're feeling. "Here's this child I love, for whom I would gladly lay down my life. I'd take the addiction off him and put in on me if I could. I want to give him his life back so he can live and be happy. Instead, I see him sad, miserable, chained, and self-destructive. I see him imprisoned by this addiction that's got him – that's got control of him – and all I want in life for him is to have freedom. It's not about his career anymore. It's not about his grades. It's not about his car. I just want him to *live*."

I get it. I *was* that kid. I was also a *father* to that kid. It's not easy, and nobody can do it for them. But freedom and a real life are *possible*. Ricky and I are living proof.

PART III
THE WAY OUT

16
CAUSES OF ADDICTION

I work with people closely in many areas of the rehabilitation process, (physical, emotional and spiritual) and that kind of intensive process is a major step to making headway against addiction. What I can do now is help you see what this is really all about, and encourage you through my own story, and through the story of my son. In Chapter 25, I describe my *Free for Life At Last: Overcoming Addiction* program, which I believe provides people an immediate, complete and confidential way to begin to overcoming addiction immediately

One of the reasons people don't get help is because of the stigma associated with addiction. When they hear the word *addiction*, people often think of driving through some bad neighborhood in the middle of the night buying crack. Sometimes that's how addiction really is – but often it's not. Getting rid of the stigma is an important step.

There are many schools of thought regarding the cause of addiction, among scholars, doctors, psychiatrists and psychologists, all lining up on different sides. Some say you're genetically predisposed. Some say it's your environment. Some say it's your personality. Some say it's the substance itself – that the drugs or gambling were too tempting.

That discussion has its place, and I'm all for finding out whatever we can about addiction in order to help people. But from another perspective, I find the discussion rather fascinating – and here's why. (By the way, this is the exact thing I tell many people whom I counsel.) Let's say that you broke your leg playing soccer. That's not good, of course. Nobody wants a broken leg. Now, let's say you broke your leg in a car accident. Okay? Also not pretty, and not desirable, but you broke your leg in a car accident. Now, let's say a guy came with a baseball bat and *clubbed* you in the leg because he was mad at you and broke your leg. Or let's say you broke your leg just tripping over the sidewalk.

That's four different ways you broke your leg. Here's my question: what could *possibly* be the difference? How could it possibly matter why or how you broke your leg? The only thing that matters is *you have a broken leg*. How it happened might be of some academic interest, or of interest to the justice system, or to history, but the only pressing question for you right now as you sit there with your broken leg is: what are you going to do about it?

Addiction is the same way. We can sit around and talk about all the reasons and causes for addiction, and that's not unimportant. Yes, there are different causes; and yes, some people can be more genetically predisposed. And yes, environment is an issue. But at the end of the day, we have someone who's *addicted*. At the end of the day, someone has "broken his leg," so to speak. Really, what's the difference? The only thing that matters is, what are you going to do about it? And if you had that broken leg, would you say, "Well, you know what? I can't get my broken leg fixed because it happened in a soccer game. Maybe if I'd broken it in a car accident, then it would be worthy of having fixed. But since it happened in a soccer game, I can't get it fixed." That's ludicrous. It's ridiculous. And yet it's often how we think of addiction.

Look, it doesn't matter how you got to that state, it just matters what you're going to do about it. It's not like you checked a box and said, "Hey, I want to wake up, ruin my life, become an addict, and throw everything away. I want to have physical, emotional and spiritual pain that I can't seem to recover from and live the crappiest life imaginable." I know that's not what happened, so never let the "how" you got addicted serve as an excuse for not taking action to address the problem.

17
MY LOVED ONE
IS AN ADDICT

It's particularly important to take a few pages to talk to those of you who are not addicts, but who *love* an addict and are trying to help him or her. I've been on both sides of it, as an addict, and as the parent of an addict, so there are some things you need to hear.

If you're the parent of an addict, or the spouse or relative of an addict, I want to tell you that blaming yourself doesn't make it better. There are a lot of reasons for addiction, and a lot of reasons why your child's or spouse's or loved one's mind works the way it does. Human beings are extremely complex entities – the most complex entities in the universe. It's not as simple as cause and effect, or A + B = C.

You can drive yourself crazy with senseless guilt. You can make anything be the cause. "Oh, I breastfed my baby or I didn't breast feed, and that's why she's an addict." Or, "I held my baby until he fell asleep or I put him down to sleep" or "We took him to the pizza place too often" or whatever.

Listen: *you did the best you could to raise your kids with the information you had at the time.* That's all any of us can do.

Sure, if people knew that lead paint was harmful to their kids, they wouldn't have let them live in the Bronx in a lead paint building for 30 years. But they didn't know back then. It wasn't their fault. You can never plan for all the curve balls the world may throw at you.

So, your loved one's addiction is not your fault. You didn't choose for your kid to become an addict. You may have been predisposed yourself. You may have even *been* an addict. You may have that trait in you, but that kid made his own decision on what to do with his life. Beating yourself up is not going to make it better, and that's something that we need to get straight right out of the gate.

This is extremely important, because many addicts use guilt to manipulate their family and friends, and continue their behavior. "It's your fault. *You* made me like this. I'm an addict because you didn't do what I wanted you to." It leaves you sitting there reflecting on whatever you think you might've done wrong, wondering what you could've possibly done better – instead of trying to figure out, how can we help our daughter or son? *She's* got the problem. How can we help her?

18
HARD TRUTHS

After working with thousands of addicts and the loved ones of addicts, over many years, let me tell you some basic, important truths I have learned. These are hard truths to hear – both for the addict and for those around him. As I've emphasized, the addiction is by no means your fault. And not all of the things I list will be true of every single situation. But they're true the vast majority of the time, and at least several of them will be true in each addict's case.

PARENTS ENABLE THEIR KIDS. Most of the time, parents will enable their children. Why would you do that? Because you love your kid. You don't like the idea of your kid being upset. You don't like the idea of your kid not getting what he wants. You don't like the idea of your kid struggling, of your kid suffering, of your kid hurting. So, out of love, we'll often enable our kids to do what they want to do. That's not always in their best interests.

YOU CAN'T MAKE YOUR KID BETTER OR FIX THEM. Huh? Why are we reading this book then? No. You can get information and facts to try to help the addict make an intelligent choice. But you can't fix it for them. I would have done anything I could to fix Ricky's drug addiction. I would have paid any amount of money. I would have traded my own place with him. I even told you about threatening his friend with physical harm. There is nothing I would not have done to save that kid's life if it was physically within my power. It was not. I couldn't fix him.

ADDICTS LIE ALL THE TIME. This is a tough one, but it's true. An addict is always going to lie. They often lie even when they can tell the truth. They may lie when they don't have to. Why? It seems to make no sense. But it's part of the addict personality. It's the addiction that's taken over. *All addicts lie.* It's a fact. Expect it.

MANY ADDICTS ARE CRIMINALS. I don't say this to dump guilt on already-guilty addicts. But if you're not an addict, it's important that you understand. The addict is probably going to engage in criminal behavior. That's right. Your spouse, your son, your daughter, who you love, is to some degree a liar and a criminal. They're breaking laws, whether it's stealing, driving under the influence, or using illegal drugs. It's the addiction acting out in their life that makes them do it. If you're complicit in covering up or denying their behavior, it makes you an enabler.

NOBODY ELSE WANTS TO BE AROUND YOUR ADDICT. Often, you'll discover that others don't want to be around your son or daughter or your spouse. They know he's an addict, and they don't want to deal with it. They don't have as much invested in the addict as you do, so in some ways they can be more honest and objective. And you know what? That's not necessarily a bad thing. Those who've been affected by an addict have every right to make that choice. It increases the addict's sense of isolation, but it can also be a wake-up call – for the addict and for their loved ones.

THINGS ARE DIFFERENT NOW AND ALWAYS WILL BE. I told you about my own life. I was going to make a life-long career as an advertising hotshot on Madison Avenue. And I told you about Ricky. He (and I) thought he was going to Berklee to become an amazing sax player. He had all this talent. But you know what? It didn't happen. Life will never be the same. He's not going to be that kid anymore. But we can be new people, with better lives and purposes and passions than we even had before. Life *will* forever be different. But it *can* be *better*.

19
HOW ADDICTION WORKS

Here are some basics, to help us down the right track to understanding exactly what we're talking about. These things are true no matter which particular way you act out or indulge your addiction (alcohol, drugs, gambling, etc.) or the manner in which someone got hooked.

Here's the dictionary definition of addiction and it's a very good one. "Addiction is the state of being enslaved to a habit or practice, or to something that is psychologically or physically habit-forming (such as narcotics), to such an extent that stopping causes severe trauma."

Without getting too technical, we do have some good science on the physical aspects of addiction. We know that addiction is a chronic disease of the brain reward function, of brain motivation, of memory and of all the related circuitry. When something goes wrong in these circuits, it has effects in every part of us – biological, physiological, social, spiritual, you name it.

So what's happening here? Our brain is wired to function in a certain way. If I gave you directions to go from my house to the store, I'd be giving you the specific path you should take to get there. That's the route. If you don't go that way, guess what? You're going to get lost.

Our brain is wired a specific way, but we know that addiction, this chronic disease, can actually rewire the circuitry in our mind, our thinking, sending thoughts which drive our actions down the wrong pathways. When that happens, we get "lost," so to speak, and we have social, psychological, spiritual and biological manifestations, none of which are pretty, and none of which are good. We know that without treatment or engagement in recovery activities, addiction is progressive and can ultimately result in disability or premature death. The brain is not an organ to mess with, and none of us are qualified to rewire the circuitry God put in there.

One thing that happens when addiction begins to rewire the brain is we lose the ability to rightly evaluate the pros and cons of our behavior. We can't properly evaluate what costs and benefits are. A non-addicted person might say, "I'd like to gamble, but I'm not going to do so at the expense of my wife and kids not having clothes and food." That's a normal way of making a decision, properly weighing one thing against another, with a good set of priorities guiding the whole process.

But the addict can't do that. She says, "No, I'm going to gamble because I'm going to do what I want. I'm going to get *what* I want, *when* I want. I'm in control. I may have some idea that it hurts the people I love, but I don't care at the moment because my immediate need or desire is more important." Or a drug addict says, "I am going to use drugs because I am going to do what I want, when I want. I'm in control... even though I know it's causing me to lose my job, my wife and my health.

Now, if you're the loved one of an addict, I want you to understand that the mindset of an addict is not necessarily that we get up in the morning and write a mantra or have a bumper sticker that says, "I want what I want, and I'll have what I want, when I want it." But that's what addiction *insinuates* and that's what it does and that's what the addict's actions are based on! It insinuates that all my needs must be taken care of, no matter the cost. As a result, *your* needs don't matter at the exact moment. I'm all about *myself*. It's not pretty. It's very narcissistic. But I'm telling you the truth. Addiction is about getting what I want and making me feel good above all else. This typically stems from low self-esteem, low self-worth, and lack of confidence in who I am.

This is (understandably) quite difficult for those around the addict to understand. The normal mind thinks, "Why can't you feel good just because of the fact you're alive, you're loved, you have a good life, you materially have the things you need?" But as an addict, those things don't make me feel good. They should, but they don't. So instead, I decide that I'm going to do all these other things that I *think* will make me feel good. Of course, none of them ultimately do. They may make me feel good for an hour, a day, a week, six months; and then, of course, they dramatically ruin my life when I realize that this addiction has overtaken me – which increases my feelings of low self-esteem, self-worth, and confidence that caused all this to begin with. There's a reason they call it a deadly spiral.

My desire as an addict is to please myself. I want to feel good. I have a situation coming at me that I can't (or don't want to) handle. There's something stressful in my life. I'm going to make myself feel better. I'll go get wasted (or gamble, or eat, or have sex, or whatever). Then I won't have to deal with it. I'll avoid it. I'll do anything I can do to escape the realities of life.

And as the addict avoids stress – surprise! – *everything* becomes more stressful. You ask an addict, "Hey, can you pick me up at the office?" You get, "Pick you up at the office! How dare you put that on *me*! How dare you! Don't you know *I* have to work? *I* have to brush my teeth! *I* have to think!"

Going to somebody's funeral. Going to the store. Going on a date. Answering the phone. All of it becomes too stressful to deal with.

Why would you need to escape the realities of life? For the addict, those things are too painful. You know, I spent a lot of years escaping the realities of life. There were things I was running away from that made me think I absolutely had to mask or cover or numb myself so that I could escape into this trance-like world. When I was in that world, I thought nobody could touch me and I was in control.

Then, when I came back to my senses and got into recovery, I realized that the very things that I was ruining my life over, thinking I had to escape from, were so minimal and so insignificant that it was stunning. Once they were exposed and I saw them, I thought, "That's what it was all about? *That* stuff?" That was it!

I'm not a psychologist, but I've been told that when you're a kid, you develop defense mechanisms in your mind that are very helpful and very valuable as you're growing up. Those strategies help you cope, they help you understand life, and they help you deal with the circumstances of your life. However often they can be an underlying cause of addiction, which is not good, if they are not discarded at the proper time, (when you are not a little kid anymore) when they have served their usefulness.

When you get older, those defense mechanisms that you had as a child are no longer necessary. Like a stroller, you needed one when you were a little child, but now you can walk on your own just fine. The last thing you want to do as an adult is say, "I need to get back into the stroller to get around." But unless we get our lens adjusted, unless we see, understand and release the coping strategies we imported from childhood, we can get lost in this trance, this addict-like focus, and eventually it changes our body and brain chemistry, and it changes our thinking. Fortunately therapy and/ or counseling can help us recognize and bring to the surface what the specific issues are in our own lives. Once an addict can recognize them, he can deal with them. I believe it's the spiritual equivalent of turning on the lights in a dark room and the key to many addicts' complete recovery!

20
THE BAIT

Addicts do what they do because of a perceived benefit. The perceived benefit turns out to be a lie, mind
you, but they're engaging in the addiction because
they feel it *gives* them some benefit.

A 2002 study in Britain examined the "rewards" of drinking. Among those classified as heavy drinkers, 91 percent said
that they experienced relaxation, 88 percent found that drinking provided them with fun or humor, 81 percent thought it
stimulated their social life, 65 percent fostered friendships
by drinking, and 67 percent felt more self-confidence when
they drink. In other words, as far as heavy drinkers were
concerned, alcohol allowed them to have more fun, improve
their dealings with other people, and made them feel better
about themselves.

Earlier in the book, I told you about my experience with
cocaine, which is fairly typical of cocaine users. Cocaine users
often in the beginning like the energizing feeling. In my own
experience, my mind was alive. Everything was intensified.
Everything was wonderful. I felt invincible, like anything was
possible, like I could do it all. I was on top of the world, I could
function incredibly, and my perceptions were sharpened.

Remember how I told you I thought if everybody did a line
of cocaine, we could solve all the world's problems? I've experienced, first-hand, every one of those feelings I described,
which are typical of the cocaine user. And I want to remind
you, it's *temporary*. It's only that way in the very the beginning. That's the trick. That's the cunningness of addiction. It
is said to be a baffling and insidious disease, cunning in its
deceit, as it will go to any lengths to trick you and trap you. It

seduces you and says, "Hey, come here. I'll be your friend. I'll give you all these great feelings, make you able to cope, and solve your problems for you."

And then, quickly, you're trapped.

Have you ever seen when a mouse trap goes off and doesn't kill the mouse, but catches it by the foot or leg? It's a horrible, gut-wrenching thing. That's exactly what addiction's like. You're trapped like a rat. You're caught. You're beat. You're defeated. You're broken, and it happens like the mouse going after the cheese on the mousetrap – SNAP! It happens so quickly.

Why do we teach our children not to take a piece of candy from a stranger? Why do we warn our kids not to get into the car with someone they don't know who's promising to take them someplace fun? Because we know that it's probably bait for something awful. Rather than taking the bait, we teach them to say, "Get away from me! I'm going to call the police and have you arrested! Get away from me! I don't trust you!"

Why wouldn't you trust a stranger? He said it was going to be a good time. He said he was going to show you something good. You don't trust him because your basic instinct of survival says he could be *lying* – and probably is. Our common sense (hopefully with some parental input) tells us that this is dangerous and that I'm not going to do it.

Yet, when it comes to drugs, we say, "Oh, okay. I'll believe your lie. I'll take the bait. Come on in here! It's great!" It's not great. It's slow-motion death. But the promise of those temporary rewards is what drives us to the drug and what makes us want to use and use.

21
NEW TOOLS

In recovery, we need to set up in our lives another system of rewards that's better or more valuable than the drugs. That system of rewards needs to include things like community, love, and passionate drive toward a purpose.

As addicts, we need to examine the circumstances and desires that drive us toward addiction. What's the place of addiction in your life? When do you resort to your addiction? What happens before you use drugs? How do you feel right before you're turning to it? What do you experience when you resort to it? What do you experience as a result of it? What results come from your addictive behavior on a long term or short-term basis? Why do you turn back to your addiction? You can start to write these things down and look at them and answer some of these questions.

This will give you some of the keys to your life. Here's what an addict using drugs might say: "It relaxes me. It reduces my anxiety. I feel as though I'm taking care of myself. It gives me a sense of control over my feelings in my life. It makes me feel more attractive to others. It lessens my depression. It provides excitement or combats boredom." Of course, you can fill in your own.

In recovery from addiction, you'll need to counter this by learning some basic coping skills. You need to learn how to deal with these social issues. You need to learn how to deal with frustration and anger, depression, anxiety, and you have to function in society. You need leisure activities.

These coping skills are not hard to learn. Remember when you learned how to drive a car? Remember how you had to study the book on the rules of the road, and then you had to pass the road test to show your proficiency? It may have seemed like a lot at the time, but after just a little basic practice, it became like second nature to you. Most of us don't think about driving while we're driving – it just comes naturally to us now. These coping skills are like that – you just need to practice them a little. There are people who can teach you, just like with driving, so you have no excuse for not taking control of your addiction.

Another essential skill for beating addiction is problem solving. Addicts generally run away from problems rather than facing them. In the place of feeling defeated, we must learn new methods to cope and deal with everyday problems. I help people with this in my personal counseling and my addiction seminars all the time. The addict needs someone to help guide and coach him through this.

It's also absolutely vital to learn how to be alone and independent. An addict can hardly even imagine this, but when you begin to recover, it's not terrible to be alone for a little while as you learn to love and appreciate yourself. One of my greatest pleasures in life now is one of my simplest ones: having a cup of tea in the morning by myself at McDonald's. I just sit there, sipping my tea, maybe reading the paper. I'm so happy just to *be*. Just to be alive, not even doing anything. Just enjoying the moment. Isn't it amazing that such a small thing would bring me so much joy?

When I was trapped in my addiction a simple joy like that would be absolutely unthinkable. Don't get me wrong – I love being with people and interacting with them. I love being part of a community in the world; but I've also learned to enjoy being by myself. I've come to love and appreciate myself for who and what I am, and that's where the joy of life comes from – and that's a key to overcoming addiction.

I understand that you may not feel that way about yourself today. You may not feel that love, and it may seem impossible. But what if I told you that there are people, and I'm one of them, who can show you the way? I hope I am helping you with this book and in my *Free For Life At Last: Overcoming Addiction* online video program, *(described in Chapter 25),* and in our live seminars, we provide many of the tools and information necessary to begin overcoming addiction immediately.

You can find many different avenues of recovery. *There is a way.* There is a path. Would you at least go take a look? If I told you there was gold in my backyard, you might not believe me, but you would at least take a look because you'd be scared to miss it. Don't miss this. It's there if you look for it.

On the other side of being able to be with yourself, you also absolutely need intimacy and supportive relationships. I once heard someone break down the word "intimacy" in a way that really struck with me: "into-me-see." Intimacy. To an addict, that's *terrifying*. We won't even look into ourselves. How are we going to let anybody else in? Establishing intimacy is essential. We don't have to be perfect. But we have to be real. We are who we are, and we have to learn to be proud of that with all our faults and all our wonderful traits, as well.

We need to have supportive marriages and families. And those who are single need supportive friendship groups.

We also need to have a purpose. This is why employment and work resources are important, and most recovery programs can help you with those things. It's important to work and derive a sense of accomplishment from what we do. Hopefully, you'll be able to work at something you're passionate about or good at. You should strive for excellence and look for a sense of accomplishment, and round it out with leisure activities, hobbies and interests – different healthy ways of relaxing and enjoying life.

I know to an addict all of this sounds impossible. But I'm here to tell you it's *not* impossible. I've been there, and I've done it. And there are millions of others. Your addiction has convinced you into believing lies. As you recover, you're going to learn how to reprogram and recondition yourself, so that you can appreciate life, and the beauty and joy around you.

22
HIGHER POWER

As an addict, I've trained myself (with the help of God and others) to think differently. I still face temptation, as do most addicts, but I want to let you see into my mind, so you can see where my freedom has come from, and how I maintain it and deal with temptation when it comes.

So when a temptation arises, here's what I've trained myself to do: I immediately think, "You know what? This addiction [cocaine, Quaaludes, placing a bet, or whatever] seems appealing right now. So let me think through the end result of that action." Already, by thinking about consequences, I'm making headway in defeating addictive behavior.

Then I walk myself through it. I tell myself, "You'll have the cocaine, and you will definitely disappear again for three days. Once you start doing one line you won't be able to stop, and you'll go through an eighth, or a quarter ounce, or a half ounce of cocaine in three days. You will lose everything that you have worked for in your life. You will lose your credibility, you will lose the respect of your family, you will lose respect for yourself, and you'll lose all the wonderful things you've done. Not only that, you will feel like complete crap, disgusting and horrible." I remember how my mind and body felt when I was coming down from doing those drugs.

So now there's some rationality happening. The thought I had about how nice that line of cocaine felt when I first did it has a counterbalance. I know there's *no question* that if I do that first line I am going to wind up back in that situation. That is a place I never want to be again. It is not even close to being worth doing the line.

I even have a board of directors' meeting with myself. This might sound funny to you, but I'm telling you, it works for me. The board consists of me and God. But sin – the devil – also attends the meeting. Everybody has a voice at the board of directors' meeting.

God says, "Jack, you don't want to do that. That's bad for your life. I have good blessings in store for your life. Trust Me and all will go well with you."

So, I say, "Okay God, that's great."

Then Satan, who is the embodiment of sin itself, speaks up and he says, "Jack, God's an idiot. What you want to do is party. You need pleasure now. Oh, you *need* to do these things. You need to gamble; you need to use drugs. You can steal; you can cheat on your wife – anything you want. Go for it! You know it's okay. God will forgive you, so you can do whatever you want."

I say, "Okay, that's interesting. You've had your say."

Then, of course, I say, "God I'm with you. I know you're right, and I know how much pain I suffered by believing the devil before."

Then we vote.

But here's the thing. Sin has no vote. He has a *voice*, he gets to speak, but he has no *vote*. God and I vote. We vote *yes* to God, and to the good things of life, and the good things of the world, and to the wonderful life He's already given me.

I'm sharing this with you because I want you to understand that whatever those urges are toward behavior that isolates and destroys you, I'm calling it sin, because that's how I relate to it. But whatever you call it, the point is, that voice may not *ever* leave your head. "Hey, come use drugs... Come gamble... You need to isolate yourself... This is your relief... I'm your buddy. I'm the object that always gives you relief and pleasure." That voice and/or desire may never go away entirely.

That's okay. He can speak all he wants, but he has no vote. He doesn't have control of my life anymore. To go back to my baseball analogies... I'm a lifelong Yankees fan. Here comes a friend's voice telling me how great the Red Sox are. You know what? He can talk himself blue. He can cite every statistic of every Red Sox player from the beginning of time to the end of time. He's not changing my mind. It really doesn't matter what he says. I'm not becoming a Red Sox fan. *I'm a Yankee fan.* I know who I am. I know which team is my team. In the same way, you need to unshakably know whose team you're on. The old adage is simple - if you have two dogs and you feed one and starve the other, the one you feed becomes strong and the one you starve eventually dies. Which will you feed... your spirit or your addiction?

I know not everybody reading this believes in God, and that's up to you. If you don't believe in a higher power, you shouldn't let that fact dissuade you from trying to find help. But I will tell you this. God was absolutely essential to my recovery, and I believe He can be to yours as well.

The reason Alcoholics Anonymous and Narcotics Anonymous tell you to seek a *higher power* is because internally you feel estranged from it, you feel separated from it. You know in your heart that you have that yearning for fullness. There's a void, there's an emptiness in the life of every person who does not have a spiritual relationship with their Creator. The

Bible says that we know He created us just by looking around. If you disagree, I can't force you to believe the way I do. But in counseling thousands of addicts, I *know* that emptiness is there. The relationship with the Creator I'm talking about is not a fearful one. You shouldn't have the attitude, "Oh my gosh, I'm going to do something wrong and there's a guy up there just waiting for me to screw up so He can slam me with a baseball bat!"

That's not how we think of our own kids. I love my kids. I love them so much I don't want them to screw up. Now, there are times I may have to discipline them because they screwed up. It's not because I'm waiting gleefully to nail them, but because I love them and I want them back on the right path to blessings, happiness and peace. That's exactly how God is with us. God loves us and wants us to have all the blessings of this abundant, wonderful life He created for us.

Not only that, but if you allow me to share the driving force in my life with you, beyond merely deliverance from addiction in the here and now, I believe you can live forever and ever in Heaven with God after your time on earth is done. Many of us look at life as a journey. We're here on earth; we have a mission on earth to glorify God, do good things and love each other. Then, when we're done, we can spend all eternity with God in Heaven. As a result of knowing that, our perspective completely changes. Sometimes we're willing to give things up now because we know there's something better later.

Here's one way to explain it to you. Let's say you go to McDonald's one day. It's lunchtime, you're starving, and you order your food: a couple of double Big Macs with cheese, some French fries and a soda. After you order, you realize, "Oh no, I left my wallet at home! I don't have any money!" The people at McDonald's don't know you, so they're not giving you credit. You're not getting any lunch today. Terrible, right?

But then we add another factor. Imagine that at the same time at home you have a freezer full of filet mignon, lobster tails and a ton of the greatest food you can imagine.

You think to yourself: "Oh man, isn't this funny. I forgot my money, they're not giving me the food, and I'm hungry. I'd really like that McDonald's lunch right now. BUT, tonight when I get home I'm having two filets and a lobster tail, because I've got a freezer full."

That's how people who have a heavenly view of life, and a relationship with God, view things. Yes, there are trials and tribulations, but we know what the end result is going to be. We know there's something far better to come, something worth waiting for. We don't want to fill up on junk food – we're waiting for the real thing. We know God loves us, and He says that all things work together for our good, so we know God is using even the difficult and painful stuff to mold us and shape us so we can have great lives. Having that perspective has helped me enormously in my recovery.

Can you imagine how amazing that is? That your home is really in Heaven, and that while there's a time on earth for you to live, 50, 60 or hopefully 100 years, when you're done, you're going to Heaven forever and ever?

To God, you are valuable, you are precious, you are wonderful, you are made with joy and love, and you were put on this earth to live a joyful, happy life. My God says we are to leap and rejoice – we are to be joyful always. He says that trials and tribulations *will* come – they're part of life – but they'll be used to strengthen us, and to make us stronger, so we have the tools we need to live this life. I've seen that in my own life, and it's my prayer you'll see it in your life.

I want to offer you personal challenge... If you've never opened a *Bible*, just pick one up and read the book of John, and ask a question of God, because I want to tell you that the God I know makes a promise – a very interesting promise. He says that if you seek Him, you will find Him. If you knock the door will be opened. If you ask you will receive. (Luke 11:9) So, that's a definite promise and commitment from God.

Ask God to reveal Himself to you, and knock and see if He opens the door to you. I have yet to meet the man that comes back and says, "Your God's a liar; He didn't show up."

I've met many that said "I won't go look." I accept that, if that's your decision. But I've never had anyone tell me they looked for Him and He didn't show up. Every addict is trying to fill a need through their addiction. Some refer to it as void or hole in your heart. God is ready and willing to help you if you want Him to and if you will let Him.

You can recover even if you don't involve God in the process. I've seen many do this. They have stopped using drugs or alcohol (or indulging their specific addiction). Yet they never seem to have the peace and joy that can only come from a one on one, individual relationship with your loving Father, God!

23
WHY NOT GO?

I n order to begin that recovery, the addicted person needs to understand that, with the help of loving, helpful friends and a suitable recovery program, the seed of renewal resides within every suffering person.

It's not embarrassing to need help. There's nothing to be ashamed of in needing help. We all need help in a lot of areas. We need teachers to help us learn, we need doctors to help us when we're sick. We need mechanics to fix our cars. The question is where to get the right help.

In the early 90's, I was editor of a magazine called *Back Pain Magazine*. This was after I had back surgery myself, and a buddy of mine who was the publisher asked me to run the magazine. (It was a pretty specialized publication, as you can tell from the name.)

What I learned from running that magazine was there were a lot of different ways to treat back pain. *A lot of ways.*

Here's what I found. If I went to the surgeon, he would say, "I can heal your back pain. I need to operate on you."

If I went to the chiropractor, he'd say, "I can heal your back pain. I need to adjust you."

If I went to the doctor, he'd say, "I can heal your back pain. Just take these drugs."

If I went to the physical therapist, she'd say, "I can heal your back pain. I need you to do these exercises."

The acupuncturist? "I can heal your back pain. I need to stick a few needles into you."

The yoga instructor says, "I can heal your back pain. You need to meditate."

The reflexologist, says, "I can heal your back pain. I just need to massage your toes."

And on and on and on.

So, through this job, and through my own experience, I learned there were many different treatments for back pain. Believe it or not, most of them worked – but not for everybody. Some of them worked for some people and other treatments worked for other people, but none of them worked for all the people. In the right circumstances, nearly every one of these treatments could be quite effective for *someone*.

The same holds true in addiction. There are different ways to treat addiction. The reason I share this experience with you is because I want you to understand that there may be one voice or one group who is talking the loudest, with the most authority saying, "This is what you need to do." That's not necessarily the case. It may be a very good idea, but just because they're talking the loudest and with the most authority doesn't mean they have the best system or solution for *you*. Perhaps it worked for *them*, and something else will work better for *you* or your loved one. There are many different ways of going at this.

What we do need you to do is to *get better!* As I learned as editor of *Back Pain Magazine*, it doesn't matter which way you gain victory over addiction and live a life of freedom. It just matters that you do it! If you want to go to New York from Florida, there are several different ways you can do it. You can fly, take a train, ride a bus, drive a car... You can hitchhike, go on horseback or walk. Some of them take longer, and some of them are much more efficient than others. I guess it depends on how motivated you are to get there, how quickly you want to get there and what you are willing to pay. They will all get you there!

The important thing is there are resources and ways available to you right now to insure you live a life free from addiction. It doesn't necessarily matter which one: a complete surrender to God, a 30-day rehabilitation program, a 12-step program like AA (Alcoholics Anonymous), NA (Narcotics Anonymous), GA (Gamblers Anonymous), therapy or counseling, intensive outpatient programs, long-term rehab programs (90 days to 1 year), the Celebrate Recovery program and there are others. There are many good options. Like back pain, not all work for everyone and some work better for some people then others. I can help you and others can, too.

24
GIVE UP

If you're addicted, please listen to me. I know you feel like you don't have it in you. I know you feel like you've tried to get sober and failed. You feel like you're at war and you're getting the crap knocked out of you. It feels like you are starving and you have no more supplies, and you've been out there forever, fighting. You're bloody and beaten. And your enemies are coming over the hill charging at you; you feel like they're going to finish you off.

But imagine this. What if the thing you've been fighting isn't the substance or the behavior, but instead it's that Higher Power? Instead of killing you, He says, "Would you like to surrender?"

Surrender? But I'm at war here!

Well, you can continue fighting that war, but where has that gotten you so far? You're bloody and beaten and starving. You're getting the crap kicked out of you. You're losing this war, big time.

Instead, the one you thought was an enemy says, "If you'd like to surrender, here's what we'll do. We'll take you in. We won't put you in prison. We'll put you to work. You can even become part of our community. Yes, we'll be your king. You don't get to be the king anymore. But our rule will be for your good. We'll take care of you and protect you – and even love you. And you'll have a much better life."

Given those options, there's no question for me. Of course I would surrender. Too often our pride and arrogance and self-reliance (which hasn't been working) keeps us away from what would make us better. And after we beat our heads against the wall long enough, we start to think there's no hope. We can never be saved, never be redeemed, never come out of this hell.

The *Bible* tells a wonderful story about a prodigal son who left his father. It's one of the most well-known stories in the Bible, for good reason. The son asked his father to give him his inheritance early. He then took off to a far country and squandered everything. He completely turned his back on his father and blew his inheritance on food, alcohol, women, parties and wild living. (Sound familiar?)

After a while, he hit rock bottom. He was poor. He was homeless. He didn't even have food to eat. Things got so desperate for him that he took a job tending *pigs* – not a dream job for a rich kid in the first century. He realized even the pigs were eating better than he was! He actually envied the pigs.

Remembering how well-fed and well-treated the laborers were who worked for his father, he formulated a plan. He knew he'd completely blown it with his father by taking his inheritance and renouncing him. But he was desperate.

He said, "Here's what I'll do. I'll go back to my father and I'll say, 'Look, I know I can't be your son anymore because I took all your money and blew it; but if I could just get hired as one of your workers in the field, that will be a far better life than I have now, and I'll be satisfied.'"

So that's what he did. He went back to plead with his father, whom he had totally rejected.

When he got near the family homestead, his father saw him off in the distance. This was a wealthy, dignified, important man. He did something that nobody expected, and that nobody in his position at that time would ever do. He ran – *sprinted* – out to meet his son and hugged him and welcomed him back.

The son told the father, "I'm not worthy of being your son. Just let me work as one in your fields like a hired hand."

The father, being the loving father that he was said, "No, you're my son, and I love you. You've come back, I thought you may have been dead, but you're alive!" He gave his son full restoration into the family, and even threw a massive celebration for him.

Jesus, the one who told this story, said *God is like that.* You may think it's too late or you're too far gone. But you're not.

There's a great story about a little kid in kindergarten that makes this point – the point I'm dying for you to see.

The kindergarten teacher gives out a piece of paper to all the kids and instructs them, "Draw a picture. Draw anything you want on this piece of paper."

The kids are happily drawing, but one little girl messes up her drawing. She tries to fix it, but that only makes it worse. She starts crying hysterically. Hysterically! She's bawling and wailing.

The teacher says, "Suzie, Suzie! What in the world is the matter?"

"I ruined it! I ruined it!" Suzie cries. "Everything is ruined! I did it wrong!" She hands the paper to the teacher, crying uncontrollably.

The teacher looks at her for a minute, and then takes Suzie's first piece of paper and puts it down on her desk. She then hands Suzie a new piece of paper.

"Here," she says. "Here's a brand new piece of paper. Start again."

That's what God is saying to you today. It doesn't matter what happened before. "Here," He says, "Start again."

God promises His mercies are new every morning (Lamentations 3:22-23) and that we should come to Him, lay our burdens at His feet and He will give us rest for our souls (Matthew 11:28-29). Best move I ever made in my life was believing God. I pray you will, too.

PART IV
FREE FOR LIFE-
OVERCOMING
ADDICTION

25
THE WAY OUT

Addiction is everywhere! Statistics show that at least one in every eight people is an addict. As you well know that number goes up significantly for college students. Most of those, if left untreated, will never live up to their potential as students or as people... a tragic shame.

I believe if a program like mine existed when I was a young man, I might not have wasted ten years of my life struggling with addiction. It is my goal and my purpose that others do not suffer as I did and as my son did, and as so many others have battling their addiction with no end in sight and with the stakes being their life, joy and reason to live. That is why I developed my program.

Free For Life At Last: Overcoming Addiction is groundbreaking and breakthrough. It was designed for addicts and their families... For addicts, so they can understand addiction and to give them the tools, information and guidance necessary to take immediate steps to overcoming any addiction issue, including alcohol, drugs, gambling, the list goes on. For parents and family members of addicts, so they can understand why the addict thinks and behaves like he does, and more importantly what they themselves need to do for their own sanity and well-being and how to help their addicted loved one.

This is a cutting edge, life changing, life saving program!!

The program consists of four modules, featuring over 9 1/2 hours of online videos. The first module is "My Story." I share my personal experience and victory over addiction, and how my wife and I endured our son's struggle with alcohol and drug addiction. The second module, "The Mind of the Addict" explains how and why addicts think and behave like they do. The third module, "The Addict's Effect on the Family" explains how the addict's behavior affects the family and what family members can and should do about it. The fourth module, "The Paths to Recovery" outlines all the different paths to recovery and ranks them in order of effectiveness.

I have no motivation to recommend one path of recovery over another. I am not affiliated with any specific doctors, recovery centers or groups. My opinion is based solely on the well-being of the people who watch my program. I bring over 40 years of firsthand experience dealing with addiction, as an addict, as the parent of an addict and as advisor to thousands of addicts and their families. The actual acting out of the addiction is just a symptom. The underlying cause of addiction must be addressed and is addressed in this video series. Therefore, regardless of which addiction you or your family member are suffering from, this program will give you the keys to becoming free from addiction, for life.

Life Solution Seminars

is a National Provider of
Addiction Recovery, Prevention & Educational Information

Our program is COMPLETE, CONFIDENTIAL AND
IMMEDIATE!

For more information or to purchase the program for
online viewing or on DVD

Go to LifeSolutionSeminars.com
Or E-mail: connect@LifeSolutionSeminars.com

Or write:
Life Solution Seminars
6574 North State Road 7, #277
Coconut Creek, FL. 33073

MEET JACK ALAN LEVINE

J ack Alan Levine, nationally known author, speaker and addiction expert, has spoken to thousands of people over the last 20+ years on dealing with and successfully overcoming addiction to find Freedom for Life. Sharing his personal story and experiences with his own addiction and recovery, as well as sharing the heartbreaking tale of his son's battle with addiction, Jack knows first-hand about being an addict and being a parent of an addict. He also knows personally how to have victory over addiction and to live a life FREE from addiction.

A sought after national speaker to companies, colleges, religious groups, business groups and other organizations, Jack has led breakout sessions on "Overcoming Addiction" at *Iron Sharpens Iron* Conferences, *Florida Men of Integrity* Conferences and *Strongman* Conferences. Jack's message based on reality, fact and faith will give you the tools you need to fight and overcome any addiction. Jack speaks often to spouses and parents of addicts and gives them valuable counsel about dealing with the realities of addiction and how to inspire their loved ones to seek help! He has also written three very popular books *Don't Blow It With God, Where The Rubber Meets The Road With God,* and *Live A Life That Matters For God.*

After being strongly encouraged to share his experience and solutions to addiction to help even more people, Jack agreed to create and develop an online program called *Free For Life At Last: Overcoming Addiction* to help all addicts and their families deal with recovery issues and outlining the clear paths and solutions available to overcoming addiction and truly finding freedom for Life. You will be spellbound as Jack shares how he overcame his addiction issues to go on and lead a happy, productive life, and how you or your loved one can do the same.

Jack is a recovering drug addict himself and the parent of an addict, so his program is based on first-hand information, experience and results. Jack believes if his program had existed when he was a young man he wouldn't have wasted ten years of his life battling addiction. Jack watched his own son struggle with drug and alcohol addiction in college and flunk out of two colleges. He is determined not to let it happen to others!

He wants to make sure people, both young and old alike, don't have to engage in the brutal and life draining ruin that is addiction by providing them with a way out... that is complete, confidential and immediate. That was the driving force and passion behind the development of this project.